THE ESSENTIAL GUIDE TO DONALD TRUMP:

(And Why I Am Sailing to Nova Scotia If He Wins)

THE ESSENTIAL GUIDE TO DONALD TRUMP:

(And Why I am Sailing to Nova Scotia if He Wins)

Kenneth F. McCallion

Bryant Park Press

Copyright © 2016 by Kenneth F. McCallion

All rights reserved. Published by Bryant Park Press

For information about permissions to reproduce selections from this book,

Email: Permissions@hopscotchhome.com or submit request by facsimile to

1 (203) 724-0820

ISBN: 978-0-9979292-1-8

Manufactured in the United States of America

TABLE OF CONTENTS

PREFACE 1

TRUMP AND THE MOB 9

TRUMP AND TORTURE 22

TRUMP AND THE MUSLIMS 41

TRUMP AND THE CHRISTIANS 52

TRUMP AND THE JEWS 57

TRUMP AND WOMEN 61

TRUMP AND THE WALL 68

TRUMP AND THE RUSSIANS 82

TRUMP AND HIS TEAM 133

TRUMP AND THE "SECOND AMENDMENT PEOPLE" 141

TRUMP AND GUNS 146

TRUMP AND THE VETERANS 148

TRUMP AND THE ELECTORAL SYSTEM 150

TRUMP, HIS CHARITABLE CONTRIBUTIONS AND HIS TAXES 155

TRUMP AND HIS BUSINESSES 165

TRUMP AND THE DISABLED 174

TRUMP, PSYCHOPATHOLOGY AND THE NUCLEAR CODES ... 179

TRUMP AND HIS WORDS 185

TRUMP, BIGOTRY, XENOPHOBIA AND RACISM 186

TRUMP AND THE ECONOMY 193

TRUMP AND HIS DOCTOR 198

TRUMP AND THE LOUISIANA FLOODING 201

CONCLUSION 203

PREFACE

Ever since Donald J. Trump burst onto the national political scene in 2015 with his trip down the golden escalator at Trump Tower, I have watched with fascination – and then mounting horror – at the havoc he has created. It is much like looking at a major car wreck on the highway. There is nothing you can do about it, but you can't take your eyes off it.

Why would one of the two principal political parties in the United States nominate for the Presidency a man so uniquely unqualified to hold that position? What does it say about the state of affairs in America today that the Republican Party would choose such an intemperate and unbalanced man as their standard bearer? How could so many of my fellow citizens vote for Mr. Trump in the Republican primaries, when the overwhelming evidence should have indicated to any reasonable and objective observer that he was a disaster waiting to happen if he was elected as our President and Commander in Chief? Why couldn't they see that this showman and pseudo-businessman turned political demagogue posed a grave danger to American democracy and our national security? What was I missing?

That is how I started writing this book. At first, it began with a shopping list of issues that I felt disqualified Mr. Trump as our next President. Then, as the list grew, and I started filling in more and more detail, it occurred to me that a short book might help my fellow citizens to understand the man better and to understand that some of the senior advisers and staff he has surrounded himself with are truly dangerous people with long histories of acting contrary to American interests and American democratic principles.

You may be asking yourself: What do I know about Donald Trump, and what new perspective or insight can I offer regarding this candidate and what it would mean for the United States if he were to be elected as our next President? Good question. So let me tell you a little about myself.

I graduated from Yale College in 1968, and from Fordham Law School in 1972. After law school, I was a prosecutor for about 15 years. During that time I served as an Assistant U.S. Attorney, a Special Assistant Attorney General with the Organized Crime Section of the U.S. Department of Justice, and as a New York State prosecutor with the Attorney General's Office and the New York State Special Prosecutor's Office.

For the last 20 years or so, I have primarily worked in private practice as an environmental and human rights attorney, with a specialty in international human rights cases. I have worked on several of the Holocaust restitution cases, particularly those that led to the settlement with the French Banks, and another with the German government and German industry. I spent a fair amount of time in Russia since I represented many Russian survivors of World War II who had been transported to Germany against their will, and then used as forced laborers under abysmal conditions. These Russian forced laborers were finally able to receive some compensation from Germany as a result of a settlement reached in Berlin after protracted negotiations. Much of my

Preface

legal work on behalf of these Russian clients took place in St. Petersburg, Russia, where President Putin got his start.

More recently, I spent several years representing the former Prime Minister of Ukraine, Yulia Tymoshenko, and other Ukraine opposition leaders, who were arbitrarily jailed and prosecuted on trumped up charges by the previous Ukraine President, Viktor Yanukovich. In February 2014, after a series of prolonged and often bloody public demonstrations, this pro-Russian and autocratic President was forced to flee Kiev for the Moscow safe haven offered by his patron, Vladimir Putin. With this regime change, Ms. Tymoshenko and other political prisoners were immediately released from prison.

Yanukovich and his cronies, including oligarch Dimitri Firtash, were the primary defendants in the human rights case that I brought in the U.S. courts on behalf of Yulia Tymoshenko and others. However, as our investigation continued, we came into possession of various documents showing that Paul Manafort (Trump's right-hand man until he resigned on August 19, 2016) was assisting Yanukovich, Firtash and others in laundering millions of dollars through various bank accounts in New York and elsewhere. Manafort was closely affiliated with Yanukovich since, over the span of many years, he had acted as chief advisor and strategist during Yanukovich's Presidential campaigns and while Yanukovich held power in Ukraine. Manafort was generously compensated for his work. The over $12 million publicly identified in Ukrainian records that recently came to light was just the tip of the iceberg regarding the financial largesse heaped on Manafort.

What was most startling about Paul Manafort's affiliation with the Yanukovich Administration was that Manafort, an American citizen, was one of the leading architects of Yanukovich's unabashedly pro-Russian stance, to the point where many of Ukraine's official positions on a wide variety of issues were virulently anti-U.S., anti-NATO and anti-Western European. Manafort's advocacy on pro-Russian issues was so blatant that the U.S. Ambassador to Ukraine felt constrained to invite Manafort to the U.S. Embassy in Kiev to remind him that he was, first and foremost, an American citizen. The Ambassador made it clear he should not be espousing positions on delicate international and political issues that were contrary to positions taken by the U.S. Despite this "little talk," Manafort continued to work for Yanukovich and his pro-Russian henchmen until Yanukovich was forced unceremoniously to flee Kiev.

Based upon Manafort's prior work in Ukraine, it was not surprising, therefore, that he has also guided the Trump campaign down the same pro-Russian pathway. This pro-Russian policy is a radical departure from longstanding U.S. policy of providing unwavering support for our NATO allies and imposing economic sanctions on Russia for its territorial encroachment on its neighbors, including Ukraine.

It was not very difficult for Manafort to persuade Donald Trump that he should signal to Russia and Putin that a Trump Administration would have no problem recognizing Russia's de facto annexation of Crimea and parts of eastern Ukraine. Trump had been enamored with Russia and its despotic leader, Vladimir Putin, for at least two decades, so it came very naturally to Trump when he questioned whether the U.S. should come to the aid of a NATO ally that was subjected to attack if that

Preface

NATO ally was not current on its NATO bills. In other words, since both Trump and Manafort were predisposed to a sharp tilt in U.S. policy in favor of Russia, their campaign partnership seemed a perfect match.

Even after Paul Manafort was forced to resign from the Trump campaign due to the revelations regarding his close affiliation with the former Ukraine pro-Russian regime, and the public disclosure of a previously secret handwritten ledger indicating that he had received over $12 million in cash "off-the-book" payments from that foreign government, Manafort continued to serve informally as a key advisor to Trump. Also, several other key pro-Russian advisors and senior staff remained with the Trump campaign organization, including Carter Page and Boris Epshteyn, a Russian emigre with close Russian connections at the highest level, who has emerged as one of Trump's chief spokespersons. Epshteyn has been particularly effective in disseminating Russian propaganda in an attempt to justify Russia's seizure of Ukraine's southern peninsula of Crimea in 2014 as only a humanitarian effort to protect the Russian-speaking population located there.

I also have learned a fair amount about Donald Trump over the years, first as a prosecutor investigating the infiltration of organized crime into the unions involved in the construction trades, such as Local 282 Teamster President John A. Cody, who had many dealings with Trump regarding Trump Tower and various other Trump construction projects.

I also dealt with Trump after I left the government and went into private practice, where I did a great deal of construction litigation before transitioning to environmental and human rights work. In fact, after completion of the Trump Tower, I served as one of the three arbitrators in the Trump Tower arbitration. Mr. Trump wanted to avoid paying the contractors who built the Tower the last 10-20% under the construction contracts because they were a few months late in completing the work. In the grand scheme of things, the delay of only a few months on a major construction project is not unusual. To put it into perspective I had worked on other cases where the construction project was years behind schedule and tens or hundreds of millions of dollars over budget. So, needless to say, the other two arbitrators and I eventually found that Mr. Trump was, indeed, contractually obligated to pay the full amount of the construction contracts. This decision doubtlessly infuriated Mr. Trump, who had a bad reputation in the New York real estate world as being a notorious "slow payer" or "no payer" on his construction projects, if he could get away with it.

Just as some reporters covering Trump and Manafort have relied, at least in part, on information and documents that I have provided to them, I also have heavily relied on press coverage for almost all of the subject matter areas covered in this book. I have tried to give proper attribution to all of these published articles I rely upon, but if I have missed any in the rush to get this book out while the campaign is still ongoing, I apologize in advance.

Finally, I should note that I am an avid sailor and know the New England coastline quite well. But I have never yet had the opportunity to sail all the way up to Nova Scotia. However, I have told my family and close friends that if Donald Trump is elected as the next President of the United States – despite my efforts and those of countless others to expose

Preface

him as the dangerously unstable con man that New Yorkers have come to know -- I plan to sail to Nova Scotia for a long, long extended vacation.

THE ESSENTIAL GUIDE TO DONALD TRUMP

1

TRUMP AND THE MOB

Since Donald Trump has repeatedly characterized himself as the "Law and Order Candidate," his close dealings with numerous mob figures and career criminals over the years bears particular scrutiny. Organized crime is the antithesis of law and order. Organized criminals make their "living" every day by breaking the law, defrauding people out of their life savings, manipulating the stock market, using fear and terror tactics to extort money from businesses, selling drugs, promoting prostitution and preying upon gambling addicts. Anything to make a buck by appealing to our basest weaknesses and worst impulses. So why is Donald Trump so close to the mob?

Trump, of course, is not the first real estate developer and casino owner to have had ties with members of organized crime. Indeed, it comes as no great surprise, that Donald Trump, as a real estate developer and as a casino owner, had dealings with the mob. However, as the Republican candidate for the Presidency of the United States, Trump's ties with an organized crime should be scrutinized much more carefully to determine exactly what the nature of these relationships are and to what extent they continue today. Just as voters who are selecting their next City Council member, Mayor or Representative to Congress voters should know whether a candidate for that office is cozy with the mob, or in the pocket of organized crime, they should be aware whether a potential next President is mob connected.

Why are past affiliations with organized crime reason for concern when an ex-casino owner is running for President of the United States? The reason for concern is that once a business person is close to the mob, it is virtually impossible to sever completely that relationship. Many have tried, but few have succeeded. Once the Mob has its hooks into someone, and that person wants to make a clean break from it, there are only two options: The Witness Protection Program or the morgue. Believe me (to coin a phrase) I know.

I was a federal organized crime prosecutor for many years during the late 1970s and early 1980s, where I focused primarily on the mob-controlled unions, such as Teamster Local 282, that dealt with the construction trades working on New York job sites, including those relating to Trump's construction projects. So I speak from a wealth of experience with business people and other individuals who became caught up in the dark web of violence, fraud, and deception that characterize virtually all mob relationships.

Other than his father, Donald Trump's primary mentor and role model during his formidable years was the legendary (and infamous) mob lawyer, Roy Cohn. Cohn had been Chief Counsel to Senator Joseph McCarthy during what was referred to in the late 1950s as the McCarthy Hearings, where Senator McCarthy called before the Senate Hearing Committee dozens of government officials, labor leaders and Hollywood scriptwriters and producers who were suspected of being "card-carrying Communists" or Communist sympathizers. McCarthy, like Trump, temporary transfixed the American public with dark conspiracy theories and fear that Communists were infiltrating every corner of the country and posed a grave national threat. Sound familiar? Trump's call for a ban on most if not all Muslims for fear that they will turn out to be terrorists seems like it was ripped from the pages of McCarthy's playbook.

Senator McCarthy's downfall finally came when he started accusing members of the U.S. military of communist leanings. The generals pushed back, with the famous public reprimand of U.S. Army attorney Joseph Nye Welch: "Until this moment, little did I dream that you could be so reckless and so cruel… Have you left no sense of decency!"[1]

Like the bully in the schoolyard, once McCarthy was exposed as having no sense of decency, he quickly imploded as the egotistical coward that he was, and America survived another crisis that threatened its democracy. No doubt America will survive Trumpism, just as it survived McCarthyism and countless other challenges, but each one of these national paroxysms of fear spread by homegrown demagogues leaves a trail of countless victims in its wake, people who are damaged and defamed in an instant with a reckless false comment. In many cases, these victims can never recover their reputations again. As the saying goes, "A lie can spread halfway around the world before the truth can get its boots on."

The Roy Cohn who counseled Senator McCarthy was the same Roy Cohn who was young Donald Trump's mentor as he grew his real estate business. After the McCarthy Hearings, Roy Cohn went into the private practice of law in New York and quickly earned a reputation as one of the top mob lawyers in the City, if not the country. Cohn operated out of a townhouse on East 68th Street in Manhattan, where clients

Anthony "Fat Tony" Salerno and Paul "Big Paul" Castellano were regular visitors. Besides getting advice on their legal problems, as a former secretary later recalled to Wayne Barrett in his 1992 book, *Trump: The Deals and the Downfall*,[2] the visits by the mob Titans to their lawyer's office allowed them to talk shop without having to worry about FBI bugs.

As reported by Pulitzer Prize-winning journalist Tom Robbins, Cohn told a reporter that Trump called him "fifteen to twenty times a day, asking what's the status of this, what's the status of that."[3]

I had many dealings with Cohn when I was a young federal prosecutor with the U.S. Department of Justice's Brooklyn Organized Crime Strike Force. He represented many of the mob leaders that we were prosecuting. In my dealings with Cohn, and as can be seen from most photographs taken of Cohn and Trump, Cohn rarely smiled, and his eyes were virtually lifeless as if he had seen many things that should be forgotten but cannot be.

It has been fairly well documented that Roy Cohn introduced the young Donald Trump to many of the organized crime figures that became an important part of Trump's life and career. It was also fairly well known, at least to law enforcement, that a real estate developer or casino operator who wanted to avoid any significant labor or union problems, or any problems with the construction trades, had to reach some accommodation with mob leaders. To do so, you had to have a go-between (often a lawyer) who could broker an understanding between the developer and the mob. Roy Cohn served Trump in this capacity.[4]

Trump got his start in Atlantic City with the purchase of a bar for $1 million, which was twice its market value from Salvatore Testa. Testa was a "made-man" in the Philadelphia mafia and son of Philip "Chicken Man" Testa, who was briefly head of the Philadelphia mob after the 1980 "rub out" of Angelo Bruno. Trump built Harrah's Casino on the land, and then Trump bought out his partner, Harrah's Entertainment, and renamed the casino "Trump Plaza."

As Wayne Barrett further describes, Trump Plaza Casino and Hotel's connections to the mob also included Nicademo "Little Nicky" Scarfo (who became boss after the elder Testa was blown up) and his nephew Phillip "Crazy Phil" Leonetti. Scarfo and Leonetti controlled two of the major construction and concrete companies in Atlantic City. Both companies, Scarf, Inc. and Nat Nat, worked on the building of Harrah's, according to the State of New Jersey Commission of Investigation's 1986 report on organized crime. Also, according to George Anastasia's book, "Blood and Honor,"[5] Scarfo controlled the bartenders' union, which represented Trump's workers in Atlantic City.

One more link to organized crime lurks in Trump's past Atlantic City dealings. He had a close association with Kenny Shapiro, an investment banker for Scarfo. According to secret recordings in 1983 of then-Scarfo attorney Robert F. Simone, Shapiro was intimately involved with bribing Atlantic City Mayor Michael J. Matthews, whose term would end in 1984 with a conviction on extortion charges.

Trump's projects in New York also required him to deal with several known Mafia figures and their companies. In New York City, several of his buildings were built by S&A Concrete Co., a concern partly owned by Anthony "Fat Tony" Salerno, the boss of the Genovese crime family. In addition to this business relationship, Trump and Salerno were both represented by attorney Roy Cohn. In his book, Barrett cites an anonymous source who confirmed that on at least one occasion, Trump and Salerno had a "sit-down" in Cohn's apartment. [6]

To help build his first big Manhattan project, the Grand Hyatt New York on East 42nd Street, Tom Robbins reported that Trump had chosen a notorious demolition company secretly owned in part, according to the FBI, by a top Philadelphia mobster who doubled as crime lord of Atlantic City. To pour concrete for the new hotel, Trump picked a firm run by a man named Biff Halloran, who was convicted a few years later for his role in what prosecutors dubbed a mob-run cartel that jacked up construction prices throughout the city.[7] For the carpentry contract, according to Tom Robbins in a Newsweek Opinion piece, "Trump settled on a Genovese family-controlled enterprise that was central to another mob price-fixing racket, as found by a subsequent federal probe."[8]

Based upon his cozy relationship with organized crime controlled unions and contractors, Trump was able to slash his labor costs by using undocumented Polish workers to demolish the Bonwit Teller building, which led to the construction of the Trump Tower. On paper, the demolition contractor was a union company, as were all of Trump's vendors at the time. But according to The Marshall Project, "Local 95 of the demolition workers was essentially a subsidiary of the Genovese crime family, and few union rules were enforced. Most of the workers were undocumented immigrants from Poland, and they were paid so little and so sporadically that many were forced to sleep on the job site. A rank and file union dissident later sued Trump for failing to pay pension and medical benefits required under the union contract. Trump denied knowing about conditions at the work site."[9]

Despite his denials, Trump, and his associates were found guilty in 1991 of conspiring to avoid paying pension and welfare fund contributions to the union.[10] So the next time that Trump rails against undocumented immigrants taking away jobs from Americans, or reminds us of the importance of securing our borders against the hordes of "illegals" trying to, no doubt, rape and pillage their way across the country, he should be asked about his historical use of undocumented immigrants. This use of undocumented workers would seem to qualify him more for Chief Hypocrite of the United States, not President. When he was just a reality TV and tabloid star from New York, there would be little reason for concern. But now that he seems serious about wanting to be President of the United States, he has to be held to account for his past actions.

Cohn may also have introduced Trump to John Gotti Jr., but it is equally likely that Trump knows Gotti as a fellow alumnus of the New York Military Academy, where well-heeled families send their problem children for a large dose of discipline. Trump's father, Fred Trump, sent the Donald packing off to the NYMA after he repeatedly got in trouble in grade school.[11] John Gotti Jr. was also sent there for a dose of military disciple. There is no evidence, however, that either of them took the experience too seriously.

In March 2016, Michael Isikoff of Yahoo News published a report that Donald Trump had close ties to a New Jersey man who was linked to the mob and gambled millions of dollars at one of Trump's

Atlantic City casinos.[12] According to the report, which cited as a source Robert Libutti's daughter, LiButti, the late horse breeder who was banned from state casinos for his alleged ties to mobster John Gotti, flew on Trump's helicopter and partied on Trump's yacht.

Questions about Trump's relationship with LiButti were first raised in 1991 when the New Jersey Casino Control Commission was investigating Trump Plaza employees' claims that the casino repeatedly pulled blacks and women off tables where LiButti was gambling. The commission fined Trump Plaza $200,000 for violating anti-discrimination laws after finding that hotel staff accommodated LiButti, who was reported to have regularly hurled obscenities and racial and ethnic slurs at blacks and women.

In one filing reported by Yahoo, regulators found LiButti called a Plaza casino staffer a "dumb c--t" and a "dumb b---ch," a black dealer "black bastard," and another employee a "Jew broad" in angry fits after losing craps.[13] Trump denied knowing LiButti. In 1991, he told a Philadelphia Enquirer reporter, "I have heard he is a high roller, but if he was standing here in front of me, I wouldn't know what he looked like." Trump's lapse of memory, however, would appear to be intentional since LiButti dropped more than $20 million in gambling wagers at the Trump casinos between 1984 and 1990. The Marshall Project notes that even despite the tremendous blow-back that the Trump casinos received as a result of LiButti's periodic meltdowns at the casinos, Trump "comped" the gambler with gifts of luxury autos, including Rolls Royces and Ferraris, as well as trips to Europe and the Super Bowl.

When casino regulators finally barred LiButti from all Atlantic City gambling, it was not because of his bad behavior, but because they ruled he was an associate of Gambino crime family boss John Gotti. Part of the evidence against LiButti (again according to the Marshall Project) "included wiretapped conversations in which he talked about flying with Trump in his helicopter and offering advice to Trump on how to run his casinos."[14]

When interviewed by Yahoo, Edith Creamer, LiButti's daughter, also sharply disputed Trump's denials of any relationship with her father. "He's a liar," Creamer exclaimed. "Of course, he knew him. I flew in the [Trump] helicopter with [Trump's then wife] Ivana and the kids. My dad flew it up and down [to Atlantic City]. My 35th birthday party was at the Plaza, and Donald was there. After the party, we went on his boat, his big yacht."[15]

As reported by the Marshall Project, and Yahoo, in a secret 1990 New Jersey police recording between LiButti and Edward Tracy, Trump's top Atlantic City executive, he said "I'm very close" with Trump. LiButti also made reference to a conversation with Trump on his helicopter, according to the transcript obtained by Yahoo. LiButti also recounted giving Trump relationship advice in the recording and told Tracy how the mogul once cut him a check to keep him coming back to Trump Plaza after he lost $350,000 on the craps tables.[16]

It also appears that Trump had a relationship with mob leader Sammy "the Bull" Gravano, who had a virtual lock on the construction trades in New York during the 1980s, and admittedly murdered dozens of people. He later entered the U.S. Marshal's Witness Protection Program and testified against dozens of mob figures, including his former boss, John Gotti Jr. Gravano then landed back in prison for running an Ecstasy drug ring in Arizona while in The Witness Protection Program. Karen Gravano, the mobster's daughter, who is a star of the VH1 "Mob Wives" reality TV show, has emerged as one of Trump's most vocal supporters in New Jersey. She says that Trump is an "old friend" of her fathers and that she is confident that if Donald Trump ends up in the White House, he would pardon her father. She told the New York Daily News in March of 2016: "All I can say is maybe he can give his old friend Sammy a f--- in' pardon."[17]

Karen Gravano has expressed shock that Trump now denies any relationship with her family. She has been quoted as saying: "Listen, at the end of the day, he was in construction in New York, and the mob ran construction." She further added that some "face time" with her father would have been unavoidable in the 1980s. In an ABC interview with Diane Sawyer, Gravano also confirmed – albeit cryptically – that Trump had to deal with him to get his building built in New York during the 1980s.[18]

Perhaps Trump's closest organized crime relationship was with Felix Sater, who pleaded guilty in 1998 to racketeering in a stock manipulation scheme involving the Genovese and Bonanno crime families. Sater, who had to wear a court-ordered ankle bracelet much of the time, played a role in some high-profile Trump projects and carried a Trump Organization business card with the title "Senior Advisor to Donald Trump."

As Rosalind S. Helderman and Tom Hamburger of the Washington Post reported on May 17, 2016, Sater worked out of an office on the 24th floor of Trump Tower, two floors below Donald Trump. The Russian-born businessman had already done time in prison for stabbing a man in the face with the stem of a margarita glass, and he was awaiting sentencing for his role in a Mafia-orchestrated stock fraud scheme. Sater and his business partners hatched a plan to build Trump towers in U.S. cities and across the former Soviet bloc. Trump liked the idea and gave Sater's company rights to explore projects in Moscow as well as in Florida and New York. As Sater boasted to potential investors, and according to testimony in a 2008 court case: "I can build a Trump Tower, because of my relationship with Trump." Sater played the "Trump Card" mercilessly, but without success.[19]

Despite Trump's frequent boast about his high IQ and excellent memory, he struggled to remember Sater in a deposition taken on November 5, 2013, in the case of <u>Matthew Abercrombie, et. al. versus SB Hotel Associates</u> pending at the time in Florida. Trump testified under oath that he wouldn't recognize Sater if they were sitting in the same room. Similarly, in a 2015 interview with the Associated Press, he said, "Felix Sater, boy, I have to even think about it."

Sater's sworn testimony painted a much different and more accurate picture in a libel case that Trump brought against a book author. In 2008, Trump's lawyers asked Sater to testify in Trump's libel suit against journalist Tim O'Brien, arguing that O'Brien's book, *Trump Nation: The Art of Being the Donald,* damaged his reputation and cost him projects that Bayrock and others had been pursuing. Sater testified that he visited Trump's office frequently over a six-year period to talk business with Trump. He recalled flying to Colorado with Trump and said that Trump once asked him to escort his children Donald Jr. and Ivanka around Moscow.[20]

Trump and his lawyers have stated that he was not aware of Sater's criminal past when he first signed on to do business with Sater's firm, Bayrock Group. However, even after Sater's background was disclosed in a 2007 New York Times article, Sater continued to use Trump Organization office space and business cards. When Trump's children Donald Jr. and Ivanka were planning a trip to Moscow in 2006, Sater said that Trump asked him to squire them around the city. Sater's criminal background became a serious problem for Trump when one of the company's largest projects, the Trump International Hotel and Tower in Fort Lauderdale, Fla., became engulfed in legal disputes after construction stalled in 2009. Outraged condominium buyers filed suit, claiming, among other things, that Trump and others had failed to tell them about the criminal past of a key member of the development team. Trump walked away from the failing project, saying he held no responsibility since he had merely licensed his name to the effort.[21]

Apart from Sater's criminal record, (which at the very least shows the Trump Organization's shoddy or non-existent record of doing background checks on its business associates,) Sater's notoriously bad temper was widely known, and must have been known to Trump. For example, a lawsuit filed in Arizona in 2007 alleged that Sater had threatened a local project partner named Ernest Mennes. According to the lawsuit, Sater called Mennes in 2006 and threatened that his cousin "would electrically shock Mr. Mennes' testicles, cut off Mr. Mennes' legs, and leave Mr. Mennes dead in the trunk of his car" if Mennes revealed his criminal past. Perhaps Trump does not disapprove of this sort of threats, having often engaged in such language himself.

As reported by Tom Robbins, Trump also dealt with Joseph Weichselbaum, another allegedly mob-connected businessman who ran a helicopter service ferrying high-rollers to Trump's casinos. Weichselbaum was living in an apartment in Trump Plaza on the East Side of Manhattan when he pleaded guilty to federal charges of cocaine smuggling in 1986. Trump was so tight with him that Trump agreed to accept helicopter service in partial payment of the rent on the apartment. Weichselbaum also maintained Trump's private helicopter. When Weichselbaum faced sentencing, Trump provided a letter to the court describing his friend as "conscientious, forthright and diligent." Weichselbaum received a three-year sentence and came home to reside in an even posher apartment at Trump Tower, where his girlfriend had managed to buy two combined apartments. When Trump was later asked in 1990 by casino officials about his letter to the judge on Weichselbaum's behalf, the casino mogul could not recall having written it.[22]

Given his close association with numerous mob figures, it is ironic that Trump, the self-touted law and order candidate, poses the greatest danger of any Presidential candidate in history that organized crime figures will have direct access to the White House if he is elected.

2

TRUMP AND TORTURE

Donald Trump has repeatedly and emphatically stated that if he is the next President and Commander in Chief, he will direct U.S. forces to torture suspected terrorist prisoners through waterboarding "and worse." He has also declared that he will violate existing U.S. and international law by issuing an executive order directing that the families of terrorists be killed ("We have to go after their families").

General John Allen, a retired four-star general, responded by saying that such an order from the President to U.S. troops would create a crisis between civil and U.S. military authorities. Since members of the U.S. armed forces are legally and duty bound to adhere to the Geneva Convention and numerous other international treaties which prohibit the use of torture, they would have to refuse the President's order.

Trump's penchant for violence and his near blood-lust for the infliction of pain extends far beyond the narrow confines of the War On Terror. Time and time again he has demonstrated that he loves to have protesters beaten at his rallies. Indeed, it has come to be part of the standard show at his rallies. During the Democratic National Convention, he openly spoke to the press about his desire to punch out various speakers who denounced him.

But what he loves most is waterboarding and other enhanced interrogation techniques. Not so much because it produces reliable and actionable intelligence, which it does not, but because in the sick and sadistic parallel universe where Trump and some of his most ardent supporters inhabit, torture just makes them feel good.

In December 2015, Trump started demanding that the U.S. target the families of ISIS members in addition to "bombing the sh*t" out of the terrorist organization. He went further in February 2016, advocating for the use of torture as a method of interrogation. "I would bring back waterboarding, and I'd bring back a hell of a lot worse than waterboarding," Trump declared in the February 2016 Republican primary debate just ahead of the New Hampshire primary. Calls for the use of torture became an integral part of Trump's talking points at his rallies, usually drawing thunderous applause. However, Trump carefully sidestepped the thorny issue that both of these policies would require the American military to obey orders that violated international laws and U.S. anti-torture statutes.

Pressed at a debate on March 3, 2016, over whether the American military would follow his order to violate international laws and the Geneva Convention to do such things, Trump insisted they'd listen to him, despite condemnation and cries of outrage from military leaders and conservatives. "Frankly, when I say they'll do as I tell them, they'll do as I tell them," he said confidently. The very next day, however, on March 4th, he reversed this position in a statement to the Wall Street Journal, saying he "will not order military or other officials to violate those laws and will seek their advice on such matters."[1]

At subsequent rallies, however, Trump reverted to his previous positions in favor of torture, no doubt because the crowds reacted much more positively to his talk about 'getting tough' with terrorist. As reported on Rachel Maddow's blog, Trump seemed particularly annoyed that the United States, under President Obama, felt the need to act lawfully. "We have laws; they don't have laws," Trump said while campaigning in Ohio, adding, "Their laws say you can do anything you want and the more vicious you are, the better." It just wasn't fair, Trump implied, that the law constrained the U.S. from descending to the same barbaric level as the terrorists.[2]

Trump's reasoning in support of his call for a return to barbarism was simple: "You have to fight fire with fire," he declared. "We have to be so strong. We have to fight so viciously. And violently because we're dealing with violent people viciously." Trump added, "Can you imagine [ISIS members] sitting around the table or wherever they're eating their dinner, talking about the Americans don't do waterboarding, and yet we chop off heads? They probably think we're weak, we're stupid, we don't know what we're doing, we have no leadership. You know, you have to fight fire with fire."[3]

In a CNN interview, Trump went on to say he intends to "change our law on, you know, the waterboarding thing" to "be able to fight at least on an almost equal basis."[4] Apparently, Trump sees some advantage in the United States abandoning its traditional values and becoming more like our enemies. This thinking seems to be at the foundations of his national security policy (to the extent he has one).

Besieged by criticism that waterboarding was illegal, Trump came up with the ingenious plan to permit the military to employ waterboarding and other "enhanced interrogation techniques" on suspected terrorist detainees without requiring the military to break the Geneva Convention and U.S. laws. According to Trump's reasoning, if waterboarding were only declared to be legal, then he would be able to order it without any nasty adverse consequences under the international or federal law.

Shortly after terrorist attacks in Brussels killed at least 28 people and injured dozens more on March 22, 2016, Trump called CNN to promote his plan to legalize waterboarding. "Look, I think we have to change our law on the waterboarding thing, where they can chop off heads and drown people in cages, in heavy steel cages and we can't water board," Trump told CNN's Wolf Blitzer. "We have to change our laws, and we have to be able to fight at least on almost equal basis."

When Blitzer reminded Trump that U.S. military leaders did not support torture and that it violates international agreements that the United States has signed. Trump retorted: "I would say that the eggheads that came up with this international law should turn on their television and watch CNN right now because I'm looking at scenes on CNN right now as I'm speaking to you that are absolutely atrocious." Trump added: "And I would be willing to bet, when I am seeing all of the bodies laying all over the floor, including young, beautiful children laying dead on the floor, I would say if they watched that, maybe, just maybe they'll approve of waterboarding and other things."[5]

Following the terror attacks in Istanbul, Trump renewed his urgent call for America to jump into the same dark muddy pit of depravity and beat the terrorists at their own game. "We have to fight so viciously and violently because we're dealing with violent people,"

Trump told supporters at a rally at the Ohio University Eastern Campus. "We have to fight fire with fire," and "we better get smart ... and we better get tough — or we are not going to have much of a country left." Trump further explained that waterboarding "and worse" would no longer be a war crime under his Administration because he would change the laws to allow torture.

Torture Under U.S. and International Law

The authorized use of torture by the U.S. military would be a radical departure from core American values and principles going back generations. For example, after World War II captured Japanese soldiers who had subjected prisoners of war to waterboarding and other forms of torture were executed as war criminals. As the Republican authority on torture, Senator John McCain, has himself noted: "It's not the United States of America. It's not what we are all about. It's not what we are..."[6]

Until Trump appeared on the scene, Republican Party leaders had condemned the use of torture, even when it came to dealing with terrorists. One notable exception was the Administration of President George W Bush. After 9/11, Bush repeatedly stated that the war on terrorism was about "values." He pledged that as it fought terrorism, the United States would always stand for "the non-negotiable demands of human dignity."[7]

However, the Bush Administration's commitment to maintaining American values and fundamental human rights in the war on terrorism proved to be nothing more than empty words. After the September 11, 2001, terrorist attacks, the Bush Administration decided to reverse the longstanding U.S. policy of condemning the use of torture; the results were disastrous for the U.S.'s reputation as a champion of democracy and human rights, as well as disastrous for all of those involved in the use of torture. It must be kept in mind that the use of torture harms not just the victims, but also the young men and women who participate in or witness the barbarism that is inextricably intertwined with the use of torture.

In June 2004, the Washington Post and the New York Times obtained copies of legal analyses prepared for the CIA and the Justice Department in 2002. These documents developed a legal basis for the use of torture by U.S. interrogators if acting under the directive of the President of the United States. The legal definition of torture by the Justice Department was changed so as to limit the definition of torture only to actions which "must be equivalent in intensity to the pain accompanying serious physical injuries, such as organ failure, impairment of bodily function, or even death." These "torture memos" also argued that actions that inflict any minor pain, including moderate or fleeting pain, do not necessarily constitute torture.[8]

The Bush Administration's response to these revelations was to take the position that these legal memoranda were only for "research," and did not signify the intent of the United States to use torture. However, it soon became apparent that U.S. troops were regularly mistreating and torturing prisoners under their control in Iraq, Afghanistan and Guantánamo Bay, Cuba. In 2003, Defense Secretary Donald Rumsfeld approved the use of 24 classified interrogation techniques for use on detainees at Guantanamo Bay. In court filings made public in January 2007, FBI agents reported that prisoners at Guantanamo Bay were chained in a fetal position on the floor for at least

18 hours; subjected to extremes of temperature; gagged with duct tape; held in stress positions while shackled, and subjected to loud music and flashing lights.

In 2004 photos showing humiliation and abuse of prisoners leaked from Abu Ghraib prison, caused an enormous political and media scandal in the U.S. and around the world. As the columnist Bob Herbert of the New York Times put it: "There is no longer any doubt that large numbers of troops responsible for guarding and interrogating detainees somehow loosed their moorings to humanity, and began behaving as sadists, perverts, and criminals."[9]

According to a previously secret 2002 memo that was released on July 24, 2008, the Bush administration also authorized CIA interrogators working abroad to use torture unless they "have the specific intent to inflict severe pain or suffering."[10] The interrogator's "good faith" and "honest belief" that the interrogation would not cause such suffering became a complete protection against prosecution or disciplinary proceedings against CIA personnel conducting such examinations. Jay Bybee, then the Assistant Attorney General for the Office of Legal Counsel, reasoned as follows in the memo:

"Because specific intent is an element of the offense, the absence of specific intent negates the charge of torture."

Another memo released on the same day advised that use of "the waterboard" did "not violate the U.S. statute making torture a criminal offense."

A third memo dated January 28, 2003, signed by then-CIA Director George Tenant, instructed interrogators to keep records of sessions that used "enhanced interrogation techniques." It was also revealed that both United States citizens and foreign nationals who were captured outside of the United States were transferred by the CIA to secret U.S. administered detention facilities, known as "black sites," with the detainees sometimes being held incommunicado for periods of months or years. CIA agents also had a "rendition" program, where they regularly handed terrorist suspects over to foreign intelligence services for the purpose of using torture techniques on these suspects, or just to make them "disappear."

The Obama Administration reinstated the longstanding prohibition against waterboarding and the use of other forms of state-sponsored torture, but the entire episode left a dark stain on American honor and forfeited much of the moral high ground that the U.S. has almost always enjoyed in the area of human rights and the protection of human dignity.

Moreover, while the use of torture undoubtedly inflicted much pain and suffering, the benefits regarding actionable intelligence were virtually nil. Notwithstanding the protestations of Vice President Chaney and other torture enthusiasts, there is no evidence that any reliable and actionable information of significant value was ever elicited through the use of waterboarding or other forms of torture.[11]

Why then, after such a disastrous experience with torture in the years immediately following the 9/11 terrorist attacks, would a Presidential candidate such as Trump even suggest that the U.S. should go down that dark road once again? The reasons are probably more psychological than practical. Sadists simply like to hurt people, and the infliction of pain on others is an end in itself. It makes one (if you are a sadist) feel good. The history of torture – especially the use of waterboarding -- bears this out and requires a brief survey.

A Brief History of Torture

What exactly is waterboarding and who invented it? As Sasha Abramsky reported in an excellent piece in *The Nation* on March 25, 2016, the use of waterboarding was developed during the Spanish Inquisition by the fanatical Grand Inquisitor Tomás de Torquemada, who sanctimoniously declared that torture had to be used to save souls and to destroy heretics. The Spanish employed *tortura del agua*, a technique that simulated drowning by the pouring of water over the prisoner's covered head. Much later, it was called "waterboarding."[12]

When Trump threatens that he will authorize the use of more extreme torture techniques as well, he has given no specifics. However, if the history of the Spanish Inquisition is his guide, the Inquisitors quickly moved from waterboarding to even more drastic methods. They tied victims' hands behind their backs and hung them from those hands by a rope. Known as the *strappado*, this technique inflicted excruciating pain and destroyed nerves, ligaments, and tendons in the arms and shoulders. When this method did not achieve the desired results, the torture teams progressed to the infamous rack, stretching the tied victim slowly, dislocating joints, and destroying muscles, ligaments, and bones. Eventually, if the victim didn't talk, their limbs were ripped off of their bodies.[13]

Perhaps this is what Trump is thinking of when he suggests that waterboarding is much too tame for terrorists and that under a Trump Administration, he would authorize the use of interrogation and torture techniques a "lot worse than waterboarding."

I am sure that if Trump assembled a team of experts to advise him on his various options for torturing terrorist suspects, they would inform him (if he doesn't already know) that the Nazi Gestapo hung their victims from meat hooks. They would tell him that partisans during the Russian Civil War that preferred to strip the skin from the hands of victims. Soviet medics under Stalin were ordered to use their skills to break the minds of dissidents, and the junta dictators of Latin America in the 1970s and 1980s perfected the technique of throwing young men and women out of helicopters and planes, some to plunge into the ocean, others into volcanoes. Or will Trump prefer to follow the lead of Saddam Hussein, who ordered soldiers and intelligence officials to pour acid onto victims, or drill holes in their feet and hands?[14]

The varieties of torture techniques are virtually limitless. So if this is the slippery slope that Trump wants to lead us down, I think that Trump should be required to explain to the American public what particular sick and sadistic kinds of torture he plans to order our armed service members to perform if he is elected as their President and Commander and Chief. Then the American voters can make the informed choice as to whether this is the barbaric path that they want the country to go down.

Torture and the Law

From a legal perspective, the prohibition against torture is firmly entrenched in customary international law, international treaties signed by the United States, and in U.S. law. As the U.S. Department of State has noted, the "United States has long been a vigorous supporter of the international fight against torture...Every unit of government at every level within the United States is committed, by law as well as by policy, to the protection of the individual's life, liberty, and physical integrity."[15]

The U.S. is a party to The Convention against Torture, which defines torture as "any act by which severe pain or suffering, whether physical or mental, is intentionally inflicted on a person for such purposes as obtaining from him or a third person information or a confession...." (Art. 1). It may be "inflicted by or at the instigation of or acquiescence of a public official or other person acting in an official capacity." The prohibition against torture under international law applies to all of the countless ways that acute pain can be inflicted. Included among the list of ways to inflict pain include; beating on the soles of the feet, electric shock, rape, near drowning through submersion in water (i.e. waterboarding), near suffocation by plastic bags, burning, whipping, needles inserted under fingernails, mutilation and, hanging by feet or hands for prolonged periods. [16]

International law also prohibits mistreatment that does not meet the technical definition of torture, such as when the purpose may be for something other than the infliction of severe physical or mental pain. It affirms the right of every person not to be subjected to cruel, inhuman or degrading treatment. Examples of such prohibited mistreatment include being forced to stand spread-eagled against the wall; being subjected to bright lights or blindfolding; being subjected to continuous loud noise; sleep deprivation; deprivation of food or drink; being subjected to forced constant standing or crouching; or violent shaking. In essence, any form of physical treatment used to intimidate, coerce or "break" a person during an interrogation constitutes prohibited ill-treatment. If these practices are intense enough, prolonged in duration, or combined with other measures that result in severe pain or suffering, they can qualify as torture.[17]

The international prohibition against torture as well as cruel, inhuman or degrading treatment also includes acts intended to cause mental distress, such as through threats against a family or loved ones.[18] As the U.S. Supreme Court has recognized, "coercion can be mental as well as physical…the blood of the accused is not the only hallmark of an unconstitutional inquisition." *Miranda v. Arizona*, 384 U.S. 436, 448, (1966) citing *Blackburn v. the State of Alabama,* 361 U.S. 199 (1960).

In 1948, the General Assembly of the United Nations inserted the prohibition against torture in the landmark Universal Declaration of Human Rights. Article 5 states: "No one shall be subjected to torture or to cruel, inhuman or degrading treatment or punishment." This ban on torture and other ill-treatment have subsequently been incorporated into the extensive network of international and regional human rights treaties. The prohibition against torture is also contained in Article 7 of the International Covenant on Civil and Political Rights (ICCPR), ratified by 153 countries, including the United States, in 1992. Prohibitions against torture are also found in The Convention against Torture or Other Cruel,

Inhuman or Degrading Treatment or Punishment (the Convention against Torture), ratified by 136 countries, including the United States in 1994.

Torture used during wartime is also a War Crime. Common Article 3 of the Geneva Conventions bans "violence to life and person, in particular, murder of all kinds, mutilation, cruel treatment and torture" as well as "outrages upon personal dignity, in particular, humiliating and degrading treatment." The use of force to obtain information is explicitly prohibited by Article 31 of the **Fourth Geneva Convention**: "No physical or moral coercion shall be exercised against protected persons, in particular, to obtain information from them or third parties."

Also, international law obligates the U.S. to prevent other acts of cruel, inhumane or degrading treatment that fall short of outright torture. Article 16 of the Convention Against Torture requires the U.S. to:

> undertake to prevent in any territory under its jurisdiction other acts of cruel, inhuman or degrading treatment or punishment which do not amount to torture as defined in Article 1, when such acts are committed by or at the instigation of or with the consent or acquiescence of a public official or other person acting in an official capacity.[19]

According to the *1999 Initial Report of the United States to the U.N. Committee against Torture*, the United States explicitly represented that the use of torture "is categorically denounced as a matter of policy and as a tool of state authority…No official of the government, federal, state or local, civilian or military, is authorized to commit or to instruct anyone else to commit torture. Nor may any official condone or tolerate torture in any form. Every act of torture within the meaning of the [Convention against Torture] is illegal under existing federal and state law, and any individual who commits such an act is subject to penal sanctions as specified in criminal statutes."[20]

The use of torture also violates rights established by the Bill of Rights, included in the Constitution of the United States. The Fourth Amendment grants the right to be free from unreasonable search or seizure, including the right not be tortured or otherwise abused by the police). The Fifth Amendment protects the right against self-incrimination (which encompasses the right to remain silent during interrogations), the Fifth and the Fourteenth Amendments guarantee the right to due process (ensuring fundamental fairness in criminal justice system), and the Eighth Amendment protects the fundamental right to be free of cruel or unusual punishment. In numerous cases, the U.S. Supreme Court has condemned the use of force amounting to torture or other forms of ill-treatment during interrogations. The court included such practices as; whipping, slapping, depriving a victim of food, water, or sleep, keeping him naked or in a small cell for prolonged periods, holding a gun to his head, or threatening him with mob violence.[21] The use of torture would also violate state constitutions, whose provisions parallel the protections outlined in the federal Bill of Rights.

Article 4 of the Convention against Torture obligates state parties to ensure that all acts of torture are criminal offenses under domestic legislation. The primary federal law that would apply to torture against detainees is 18 U.S.C. 242, which makes it a criminal offense for any public official to willfully deprive a person of any right protected by the

Constitution or laws of the United States. Also, Title 18 of the United States Code, Section 2340, makes torture a federal crime. The code defines torture as an act committed by a person acting under the color of law specifically intended to inflict severe physical or mental pain or suffering (other than pain or suffering incidental to lawful sanctions) upon another person within his custody or physical control.

Some commentators have suggested that the right not to be tortured only applies to U.S. citizens, but this is not the case under international law. The right not to be subjected to torture is considered to be universal, and not limited by citizenship or nationality. No detainee held by U.S. authorities within the U.S. may be tortured, regardless of nationality, and regardless of whether the person is deemed a combatant or not, may be tortured. 18 U.S.C. 2340 and 2340A. Under U.S. federal law, it becomes a bit trickier, since while the United States Code prohibits the torture of a U.S. national outside the U.S., it is silent on the issue of a non-U.S. citizen being held outside the U.S. 18 U.S.C. 2340A. However, all applicable international laws – which universally condemn torture regardless of nationality or citizenship -- would apply to U.S. officials and employees operating abroad, and the torture of non-U.S. citizens abroad would probably be in violation of the Convention against Torture and the Geneva Conventions.

U.S. courts have constructed special rules, known as "exclusionary rules," to diminish the likelihood of coerced testimony. They have, for example, ruled that coerced statements are not admissible at trial, whether they are deemed compelled in violation of the Fifth Amendment's privilege against self-incrimination or "involuntary" in violation of the right to due process. The U.S. Supreme Court in 1966 also established a rule requiring the police who seek to question detainees to inform them of their "Miranda" rights to remain silent and to have an attorney present during the questioning. *Miranda v. Arizona*, 384 U.S. 436 (1966). These Miranda rights were precipitated, in large measure, by the continuing police practice of using physical force to extract confessions, including cases where the police beat, kicked and burned with lighted cigarette butts a potential witness under interrogation.

Torture is also prohibited under the U.S. Uniform Code of Military Conduct. The UCMJ is a federal statute that prohibits U.S. armed forces from using torture to get information. The code specifically prohibits, among other things; engaging in cruelty, oppression or maltreatment of prisoners (art. 93), assaulting prisoners (art. 128) (a prohibition that includes a demonstration of violence that results in reasonable apprehension of immediate bodily harm), and communicating a threat to injure a detainee wrongfully (art. 134).

U.S. military leaders have almost universally condemned Trump's fixation with torture as a weapon against terrorists. For example, at the Democratic National Convention in July 2016, retired United States Marine Corps Gen. John Allen emphatically declared that "our armed forces will not become an instrument of torture."

Leaving aside the fact that torture is a violation of the Geneva Conventions and is considered a war crime under both U.S. and international law, and leaving the ethics and morality of it, the plain truth is that waterboarding and other forms of torture just don't work, no matter how good it makes you feel. As John McCain has stated: "[I]t doesn't work. Because if you inflict enough pain on someone that person will tell you whatever they think that you want to hear in order to make the pain stop."[22] McCain knows what he is talking about because, after being subjected to days of torture while being held captive in North Vietnam, he wrote out a confession, but deliberately included errors and communist buzzwords to make it plain he was writing under duress. He also gave false answers to questions, like naming players on the Green Bay Packers and saying they were members of his squadron.[23]

The simple truth is that torture and enhanced interrogation techniques are not a particularly effective law enforcement technique or a way of dealing with terrorists. I spent many years as a federal and state prosecutor, and during that time frame, I had the opportunity to work with many experienced and dedicated federal, state and local law enforcement agents and officers, both in this country and abroad. The nearly universal consensus among law enforcement officers and government agents was that critical information and admissions are more likely to be elicited through the patient, persistent and professional interrogations, not through physical abuse or inhuman and degrading treatment. Indeed, most experienced interrogators recognize that torture is not only immoral and illegal but ineffective and unnecessary.

It is known among law enforcement officers, as well as in the medical community, that people who are being tortured will say anything to stop the pain, and the "information" obtained as a result of the infliction of pain is, more likely than not, false and unreliable.[24] Oliver Ravel, former deputy director of the FBI, has stated that "people will even admit they killed their grandmother, just to stop the beatings." [25]

Indeed, the unreliability of forced confessions was one of the principal reasons that U.S. courts initially prohibited their use.

Trump's blood lust to torture people ignores the practical issue that waterboarding in itself would not help win the fight against ISIS, considering that it is not a technique that can be used effectively on a battlefield. As Trump has repeatedly pointed out, ISIS itself uses torture and murder, but it does so to keep captive populations in line, not as a means to gather actionable intelligence or as a tool to fight battles. Terrorist organizations torture for the sheer terror of it. Trump apparently has the same objective, which is to spread fear and terror through the use of torture, demonstrating that America itself has become a state-sponsor of terror and is as brutal as ISIS.

The U.S. commitment against the use of torture should not be abandoned. Indeed, it must be deepened as the world watches how the U.S. responds to the challenges before it. If the U.S. were to condone torture by government officials or foreign governments in its fight against terrorism, it would betray its principles, laws, and international treaty obligations. It would irreparably weaken its standing to oppose torture elsewhere in the world. And it would provide a handy excuse to other governments to use torture to pursue their national security objectives.

In short, the use of torture is not only immoral and illegal, but also ineffective as an interrogation technique. Donald Trump's call to "fight fire with fire," although superficially attractive to many of his countrymen (and even some women), in the end would only debase American values and lower the U.S. to the same barbaric level as the terrorists with whom we are competing for the hearts and minds of all of the world's citizens. When America is seen as the champion of liberty, human rights and respect for the rule of law, it is at its strongest. When it is considered to be a barbaric superpower that is willing to use state-sponsored mass torture as a means of keeping its power and privileged position in the world through a reign of terror, America is at its most vulnerable. All empires throughout history who have sought to maintain their power through mere brute force have ended up in the dustbin of history. Trump's vision would likely lead America to the same calamitous result.

3

TRUMP AND THE MUSLIMS

Early on in his campaign for the Presidency, Donald Trump proposed a ban on all Muslims entering the U.S., with the possible exception of Muslims who are already U.S. citizens, members of the U.S. military seeking legal immigration status here, or personal friends of Trump who happen to be Muslim.

In December 2015, Trump first raised the issue by calling for "a total and complete shutdown of Muslims entering the United States." He later amended his stance in an interview with Fox News, saying the 5,000 Muslims serving the United States military would be exempt from the ban and allowed to return home from overseas deployments. He also suggested that current Muslim residents, including his "many Muslim friends," would be exempt too, and able to come and go freely. In mid-May, 2016, Trump softened his proposal for the first time, stating that it was just a "suggestion" and that it would only be a temporary ban "until we find out what's going on." Other conflicting messages followed from the Trump campaign.

After the terror attack at the Orlando nightclub, Trump appeared to modify the proposal to de-emphasize a ban based solely upon religion (*i.e.* all Muslims) and to emphasize where the potential immigrants would be coming from. He said that if he's elected, he would "suspend immigration from areas of the world where there's a proven history of terrorism against the United States, Europe or our allies until we fully understand how to end these threats."[1] The Trump campaign, though, quickly backtracked, stating that the ban would indeed be religiously based, and would be a ban on Muslims. However, NBC News reported that in late May 2016, Trump's acting Campaign Manager Paul Manafort said the current status of the Muslim ban policy was, "where there is terrorist activity — Syria or Iraq — we will temporarily suspend immigration until we can establish a vetting system in which we can identify who people are who are coming in."[2]

Neither Manafort nor Trump specified how the proposed "vetting system" would be any different than the current nine-step vetting system for refugees being implemented by the Obama Administration. Trump later said that the ban would call for "extreme vetting." He did not specify what that meant, leaving some commentators to speculate that perhaps a Trump Administration would use waterboarding or even more extreme "enhanced interrogation methods" on applicants for admission into the U.S.

Thus the Trump campaign has zigged and zagged on the issue of banning Muslims from entering the U.S., just as he has on a number of other vitally important issues. The only real consistency in his statements on the subject has been an almost palpable desire to exploit the undercurrents of public hysteria and xenophobia triggered by the domestic terrorist acts in San Bernadino and Orlando that were carried out by Muslim residents and U.S. citizens within the U.S.

The Ban on Muslims and the Law

Once Trump announced his "Muslim ban" proposal, the general reaction in the media and among most constitutional experts was to declare immediately and categorically that such a ban would be unconstitutional. They argued that it was prohibited by the First Amendment protection of Freedom of Religion, or the Fourteenth Amendment's "Due Process Clause," which bars the states from depriving "any person" of their property without "due process of law." However, the answer to the question as to whether such a ban is constitutional or not is more complicated.

To address this issue from a purely constitutional perspective, we must put aside for the moment consideration of whether it makes practical, moral or ethical sense to impose a blanket ban on 1.6 billion people from entering the U.S. based solely upon their religious beliefs. Nor is the constitutional question the same question as whether such an action is consistent with fundamental American values and heritage, as summed up by the Statue of Liberty's promise to generations of poor and oppressed people around the world [3] ("Give me your tired, your poor, your huddled masses yearning to be free....").

The constitutional issues do not necessarily take into account the fact that our country was primarily built by immigrants seeking refuge from religious oppression. Groups such as the Puritans, the Quakers, the French Huguenots came to America because they were fleeing religious oppression elsewhere, just as Muslim Shia refugees from Iraq and Syria have been seeking asylum in the U.S. as a result of persecution by Muslim Sunni terrorist groups such as ISIS.

As we have sadly learned throughout U.S. history, there is often a disconnect between what is legal or constitutional and what is right and moral. Some of the darkest stains on the American soul have resulted from decisions that were found to be legal and constitutional, but nevertheless constituted outrageous deprivations of fundamental human rights. For example, slavery was legal in parts of the United States up until the Civil War, despite the fact that by 1860, virtually no one argued that it was morally justifiable. Several decades later, during the 1890's, in response to public hysteria over the "Yellow Peril" of Chinese immigration on the West Coast, Congress enacted legislation, known as the Chinese Exclusion Act of 1882, which effectively banned Chinese immigration. In *Chae Chan Ping v. United States*, 130 U.S. 581, decided by the U.S. Supreme Court on May 13, 1889, the Court upheld the Scott Act of 1888, an addendum to the Chinese Exclusion Act, finding that such blatantly discriminatory legislation was, nevertheless, constitutional. The Court relied upon the so-called "plenary power doctrine," a legal concept articulated by the Supreme Court, acknowledging that Congress and the Executive Branch have tremendous authority and discretion over immigration laws, and giving great deference to Congressional legislation dealing with immigration. The Chinese Exclusion Act was not repealed until 1943, during World War II.

Similarly, in *Korematsu v. United States*, 323 U.S. 214, a case decided in 1944, the U.S. Supreme Court upheld the constitutionality of Executive Order 9066, which was issued by President Roosevelt in acquiescence to West Coast hysteria regarding the perceived "threat" of an imminent invasion by the Japanese. Over 100,000 innocent Japanese-Americans were herded into internment camps following Pearl Harbor.

This regrettable ruling was recognized by many Americans at the time, and by post-World War II generations, as being morally repugnant and wholly inconsistent with fundamental American values.

This ban on Chinese laborers and the incarceration of Japanese-Americans, however, was based solely on ethnicity and national origin, not religion, and there does not appear to be any Supreme Court case that squarely addresses the constitutionality of such a ban based purely on religious grounds. There is no question that the U.S., as a sovereign nation, has virtually an unfettered right to decide who enters the country and who is eligible for citizenship status. Congress has the power to determine who may become a citizen and has broad powers over foreign commerce. The President and the Executive Branch also have broad powers to manage international relations and to control and secure the nation's borders.

The most recent case that is directly relevant to the issue of whether a broad ban on Muslim immigration may legally be imposed is the 1972 Supreme Court decision in the case of *Kleindienst v. Mandel*, 408 U.S. 753 (1972). There, the Court upheld the Executive Branch's refusal to allow a Belgian scholar who subscribed to a Marxist political philosophy from entering the U.S. to give a series of lectures. In a 6 to 3 split decision, the Supreme Court reluctantly declined to second-guess the Executive Branch's decision to ban Mandel based upon his political philosophy.

This *Mandel* decision, however, should not be interpreted as giving a clear green light to a ban on all Muslims from entering the U.S. because the *Mandel* decision also rejected the argument made by the

Executive Branch that U.S. courts do not even have the power to review such decisions. Also, the Court found that the Executive Branch's reasons for excluding Mandel were "facially legitimate and bona fide." Thus, it left open the door to a possible future finding by the Supreme Court that there is no rational basis for a blanket immigration ban on all Muslims.

The power of Congress and the President to ban entire groups based on national origin or religion is not unlimited under the Constitution. Some portions of the Constitution only protect "citizens," but other relevant sections were designed to protect all "persons" or "people," not just citizens. The First Amendment, for example, speaks of "people," not "citizens," and thus protects the right of all individuals to exercise Freedom of Religion and Speech. A ban on Muslims would also arguably violate the plain language – or at least the spirit -- of the Equal Protection Clause of the Fourteenth Amendment, which prohibits state governments from denying any "person" the equal protection under the law. [4]

It should also be kept in mind that there have been many proposals in the past to ban "foreigners" of one ilk or another, and with the few notable exceptions previously mentioned, such isolationist and xenophobic views have never been implemented. Throughout U.S. history, there have been "Nativist" movements, whereby American groups and even political parties have sought to lift the drawbridge into the U.S. by trying to bar all further immigration into the country.

If there is any clear lesson in American history, it is that successive waves of immigration have infused this country with the dynamic energy that has built the U.S. into the economic powerhouse that it is today, and in all probability, present and future immigration will continue to provide this same kind of energy. Just take a walk around virtually every American city or town. Take a ride in a taxicab (or Uber), dine at a local restaurant, take notice of who is mowing the lawns, and -- more likely than not -- you can see the faces of immigrants doing the necessary work that native born Americans chose not to do.

One important legal question is that if President Trump made good on his promise to ban Muslims from the U.S., who would have legal "standing" to challenge such a policy. Certainly, a Muslim outside the U.S. would not have the right to mount such a challenge since no foreign national has a constitutional "right" to enter the U.S. In all likelihood, a legal suit would be commenced by one of the thousands of Muslim refugees from Iraq and Syria who are already in the U.S. and who have sought asylum. Since they are already in the U.S., and there is a substantial body of law already in place recognizing the due process rights of detainees in deportation cases, they would be in a strong position to argue that there is no legal or even rational basis for deporting them. Moreover, given their physical location on U.S. soil, these Muslims could also claim that they have an enormous personal stake and "property interest" in remaining here in the U.S.

Given the fact that legal scholars and Supreme Court justices must be painfully aware of the Court's tragic record of jurisprudence upholding blatant discriminatory legislation targeting specific foreign groups, it would be expected that this Supreme Court would take a more enlightened and critical view of any legislation or executive action to ban all Muslims from entering the U.S.

As H.L. Menchen famously said: "Nobody ever went broke underestimating the intelligence of the American people." Hopefully, the same will not be said about the current or future Supreme Court if it is called upon to review an Executive Order by President Trump banning all (or most) Muslims from entering the U.S. But only time will tell. In the meanwhile, it is important to recognize that the question of whether Muslims may be barred from entering the U.S. solely based on their religion is not just a legal and constitutional issue, but also a fundamental moral and ethical one that may define what it means to be an American for generations to come.

Trump Versus the Muslim Gold Star Parents

On July 29, 2016, Khizr Khan, the father of deceased Army Capt. Humayan Khan electrified the Democratic National Convention with a powerful speech that sharply rebuked Donald Trump for his proposal to temporarily ban Muslims from entering the United States.

Captain Khan, a practicing Muslim who joined the U.S. Army after the September 11th terrorist attacks on U.S. soil, was killed when a suspicious vehicle approached Khan's infantry unit in Iraq. He told his troops to get back even as he rushed forward. When the car exploded, Khan was killed on the spot, but his unit was unharmed.

Khizr Khan, Captain Khan's father, made his national debut on the stage of the Wells Fargo Center in Philadelphia with a stinging rebuke of Trump's worldview that all Muslims should be viewed with suspicion, even Muslim Americans who were serving their country. "Donald Trump," Mr. Khan roared from the stage. "You're asking Americans to trust you with their future. Let me ask you: Have you even read the United States Constitution? He then pulled out the worn booklet containing the U.S. Constitution from his jacket pocket. "I will gladly lend you my copy," [5] Khan said, thrusting the Constitution into the air as the arena broke out into thunderous applause.

Any other public figure in the United States would have left it alone. When a "Gold Star" parent of a fallen U.S. military war hero speaks, criticizing you, the unwritten rule has always been to leave it alone. If you respond at all, you must do so by first acknowledging and thanking the deceased warrior and his family for their service to the country and the ultimate sacrifice that they offered.

But this was not the Trump way of dealing with criticism, no matter how sacrosanct the source of that criticism. After all, this was the Donald Trump who sent shock waves through the media and throughout America by suggesting that Senator John McCain was not a true war hero because the only thing he had done was to get his plane shot down over North Vietnam and then get captured.

The following Sunday, Trump counterattacked during an ABC interview: "Who wrote that? Did Hillary's scriptwriters write it?" He added: "I think I've made a lot of sacrifices. I work very, very hard." In other words, Trump was equating Captain Khan's sacrifice of his life for his country to hard work on a business deal. Or maybe Trump was thinking of his heroic battle against STDs.

Not content with taking a swipe at Mr. Khan, Trump then started in on Captain Khan's mom. "If you look at his wife, she was standing there. She had nothing to say. She probably -- maybe she wasn't allowed to have anything to say. You tell me."[6] The interview drew instant negative responses from Democrats and Republicans alike. Let it never be said that The Donald can't bring people together. Even GOP leaders said it was unacceptable for the party's nominee to go after a Gold Star family.

Trump continued to pour gasoline on the flames through his Twitter account. "Mr. Khan," he tweeted, "who does not know me, viciously attacked me from the stage of the DNC and is now all over T.V. doing the same - Nice!"[7] Trump's questioning as to why Mrs. Khan didn't speak gave her a clear opening to speak out. She published an opinion piece in *The Washington Post,* explaining her silence on stage that night: "Without saying a thing, all the world, all America, felt my pain. I am a Gold Star mother. Whoever saw me felt me in their heart."[8]

Khizr and Ghazala Khan then appeared for a joint interview on CNN's "New Day," where Mr. Khan accused Trump of "ignorance and arrogance." Khan also warned that Trump's attacks on Muslims were boosting terror recruitment. Khan said it was "good Muslims" who were the ones who could help stop terror and make American safer. "We are the solution to terrorism," Khan told CNN.[9]

Shortly after that, the White House weighed in with an implicit rebuke of Trump, saying that Gold Star families deserve only "honor and gratitude" for their loved ones' service. Speaking aboard Air Force One, spokesman Eric Schultz wouldn't provide a specific response to Trump's comments about the Khan family. But he said honoring Gold Star families should rise "above politics." "Families who make the ultimate sacrifice for this country's freedom and this country's safety deserve nothing but our nation's honor and gratitude and deepest respect," Schultz said.[10]

Sen. John McCain issued a very personal statement, rebuking Trump for his comments about the Khans and acknowledging their son Humayun's sacrifice. McCain noted that his son also served in the Iraq War and that the McCains have been serving in the US military for hundreds of years. "It is time for Donald Trump to set the example for our country and the future of the Republican Party," McCain said. "While our Party has bestowed upon him the nomination, it is not accompanied by unfettered license to defame those who are the best among us."

We will have to wait until election day to see whether Donald Trump's gamble to exploit America's potential Muslim-phobia pays off or not Hopefully not.

4

TRUMP AND THE CHRISTIANS

During the Republican primary season, Donald Trump announced: "I am an evangelical. I'm a Christian. I'm a Presbyterian." However, on another occasion, he stated that he wasn't sure he had ever asked God for forgiveness, as he doesn't "bring God into that picture." He soon backtracked, but his initial statement seemed to have the ring of truth about it.

We know that Trump is at least a nominal Christian, in that he was born into a Christian family. But is he a true follower of Christ? As a presidential candidate, is he at least trying to follow the teachings of Christ and to walk in the footsteps of Jesus? No one can truly look into the heart of another. All we can do is to draw conclusions from another person's actions.

Which brings us the question: What does it mean to be a Christian? It is not really that complicated, but it is powerful, which is one of the reasons why this humble spin-off from Judaism two thousand years ago has been so successful. Of all the Christian Commandments, the greatest of them is to "Love Thy Neighbor As Yourself." The virtues of charity and humility also play a significant role in the Christian faith.

All of us are failed human beings and never completely live lives that are consistent with the teachings of the scriptures, but at least we try (sometimes).

TRUMP AND THE CHRISTIANS

Do Donald Trump's words and actions demonstrate that he is trying to follow the Christian teachings? Does he try to love his neighbor as much as he loves himself?

The clear answer, unfortunately, seems to be that Mr. Trump's ego and self-adoration are so enlarged that he could never love his neighbor as much as he loves himself, even on his best day. The demeaning and belittling way that he treated his competitors in the Republican primary, his rants against "Crooked Hillary", his exhortations for his supporters to use violence against demonstrators at his rallies, his plan to fight terrorism with torture, and so on, do not appear to exhibit any degree of Christian love or charity, at least from this Christian's perspective.

Trump continually boasts that, if he is elected President, he will direct that the family members of any terrorist should be killed. This barbaric policy would not only be unlawful under U.S. and international law, but it is also would directly contradict Christian beliefs as to what constitutes a Just War. Under Just War theory, moral principles must be followed, including the moral imperative of not intentionally killing innocent civilians. Just because a family member may be a terrorist cannot make all relatives of the terrorist targets for revenge killings. Such a concept is repugnant not only to Christian beliefs but the beliefs of all other faiths, as far as I am aware.

So why do so many Christians support Trump? And why do some Christian leaders portray him in such glowing terms that you would think we are experiencing the Second Coming? For example, two of Donald Trump's most enthusiastic supporters are Jerry Falwell Jr., President of

Liberty University, which claims to be the largest Christian University in the world, and Reverend Robert Jeffress, a pastor and televangelist. In a recent opinion piece in *The Washington Post*, Falwell called Trump, without any analysis, a "leader with qualities that resemble those of Winston Churchill."[1] Really?

As Peter Wehner wrote in the conservative bible, the *National Review*, on August 25, 2016, Falwell's remarks showed a complete lack of understanding of Churchill, who "possessed extraordinary knowledge of history and policy", and Trump, who "is the most ignorant major-party candidate in U.S. history."[2]

In the *National Review*, Wehner also challenged Falwell's praise of Trump for his "kindness" and "generosity":

> What a curious way to refer to a man who has mocked a former prisoner of war, the grieving mother of a war hero, and a reporter with a physical disability. Trump likened Ben Carson's "pathology" to that of a child molester, ridiculed Carly Fiorina's looks, made menstruation jokes about Megyn Kelly, called her a "bimbo," and called women in general "fat pigs," "dogs," "slobs," and "disgusting animals." He humiliated his first wife by engaging in a very public affair. As for his purported generosity, we know he lies about his charitable giving. [3]

Wehner also took Trump to task for having suggested that President Obama was the "founder" of ISIS. It is one thing to challenge a President's policies and quite another to say that the President acted "with malice aforethought" and to accuse him of treachery and treason.

As Wehner explained, "the Christian faith [should not] be used as a blunt, political weapon"; rather, it should guide us to "a commitment of justice, to treating people, including and especially the weak and vulnerable, with dignity and respect, speaking truth to the powerful instead of acting as courtiers to them, neither slandering opponents nor placing trust in princes...."4

On March 4, 1865, Abraham Lincoln, perhaps the greatest of all Republican Presidents, gave his Second Inaugural Address. Only one month later, he would be assassinated, but on this day, when he was sworn in as President for the second time, the Union was wrestling with the issue of how to deal with a defeated and prostrate South. Many advocated that the country should seek retribution from the Southern states for the terrible suffering and devastation caused by their Secession. President Lincoln resolved to follow a different path -- a path of reconciliation, of Christian charity and forgiveness; the same principles and virtues and character that had made America great for a century already, and which would make it great for centuries to come.

> With malice toward none, with charity for all, with firmness in the right as God gives us to see the right, let us strive on to finish the work we are in, to bind up the nation's wounds, to care for him who shall have borne the battle and for his widow and his orphan, to do all which may achieve and cherish a just and lasting peace among ourselves and with all nations.

One would never expect Candidate Trump to measure up to an Abraham Lincoln, but it would be nice if the Republican candidate at least acknowledged that at one time, long, long ago, the Party of Lincoln stood for the bedrock moral and ethical principles that have guided generations of Americans. Unfortunately, Trumpism represents a deviation from that noble tradition.

5

TRUMP AND THE JEWS

It is unlikely that Trump is personally an anti-Semite. His daughter, Ivanka, converted to Judaism when she married her husband, Jared Kushner, who is Jewish.

However, much of Trump's core support comes from a slice of white *Homo Erectus Americana* that is racist, xenophobic (fearful of anything foreign, for those who dislike big words), bigoted and generally resentful of most social and demographic trends over the past 20 years. Along with this package goes anti-Semitism.

As a result, Trump has surrounded himself with people who generally reflect his "base", which inevitably means that if you dig not too far below the surface, you will find the conviction that Jews control far too much of the wealth and power in this country, and that Trump's campaign to "Take Back America" includes, among other things, a desire to take it back from minorities and the Jews. This is a sad but true reality.

Case in point. The Trump campaign hired Steven Bannon to take over as campaign chairman. The media starting digging into his past and struck pay dirt.

The *New York Daily News* reported Friday, August 26, 2016, that Bannon's ex-wife said in a 2007 court statement that Bannon didn't want their twin daughters attending a school because too many Jews attended. "The biggest problem he had with Archer [School for Girls in Los Angeles] is the number of Jews that attend," she said in her statement, which was reported in the *New York Daily News*. "He said that he doesn't like the way they raise their kids to be 'whiny brats' and that he didn't want the girls going to school with Jews," Bannon's ex-wife wrote, according to the Daily News.[1]

Bannon denied making the statement, and the Trump campaign stood by its man. Nevertheless, this was only one of many troubling incidents where the Trump campaign has had to "walk back" what has generally been considered to be anti-Semitic comments.

One Trump campaign ad featured the image of the Star of David, superimposed on dollar bills and the picture of Hillary Clinton. Many Americans, including many American Jews, saw this picture as fundamentally anti-Semitic and neo-fascist.[2]

Most American Jewish voters are inclined to vote for Mr. Trump's opponent, not so much because Hillary Clinton has been a longstanding staunch supporter of Israel, which she has been, but because Trump, quite frankly, terrifies them and much of his support comes from white supremacist, neo-fascist Jew-haters.[3]

Donald Trump claimed that the new Republican Party platform is "the most pro-Israel of all time." But that, of course, depends on your perspective. As *Haaretz,* an Israeli newspaper, reported on August 28, 2016, some people, including most American Jews, would argue that the proposed platform is, in fact, profoundly anti-Israel. It reneges on previous GOP support for a two-state solution, first enunciated by President George Bush in 2002. According to *Haaretz*, many Jews, both in the U.S. and in Israel, view it as the only way to salvage Israeli democracy and to ensure the country's long-term well-being.[4]

TRUMP AND THE JEWS

The *Haaretz* article further notes that only 3-4 months ago Trump told *The New York Times* that he supported the two-state solution, commenting that "Trump discards past positions like most people change underwear."[5]

Trump has apparently entrusted his Israel affairs to two long-time advisers and attorneys, David Friedman and Jason Greenblatt, who are both friendly to the Jewish settlement movement and suspicious of those who support a two-state solution. Based on the analysis in *Haaretz*, this position places them somewhere between right and extreme right on the Israeli political spectrum, between Benjamin Netanyahu and Naftali Bennett.

However, most American Jews support a two-state solution, as polls have consistently shown. Contrary to Israelis, who back a two-state solution in theory but don't believe in it in practice, 61 percent of American Jews believe that an independent Palestinian state can live peacefully with Israel side by side.[6]

As *Haaretz* analyzed Trump's position, it decided that Trump was either "simply clueless" and knew nothing about what most American Jews really believed, or that Trump was basically writing off most of the American Jewish voters and, instead, seeking support among Orthodox Jewish voter, who are generally opposed to a two-state solution and support the West Bank settlements, and Evangelical Christians, many of whom view the two state-solution as somehow anti-Israel.[7]

No matter what the motivation is for Trump and the Republican platform to abandon their longstanding support for a two-state solution, and Trump's reluctance to unequivocally repudiate the virulently anti-

THE ESSENTIAL GUIDE TO DONALD TRUMP

Semitic and racist comments of his most rabid supporters, American Jewish voters have many good reasons to feel queasy at the prospect of a Trump presidency.

6

TRUMP AND WOMEN

Claire Cohen of *The Telegraph* documented the offensive, sexist and derogatory statements that Donald Trump has made in recent years about women.[1] One of the most memorable incidents was when Trump made menstruation jokes about Megyn Kelly of Fox News, and then calling her a "bimbo." But he is also prone to defame women, in general, referring to them generally as "fat pigs," "dogs," "slobs" and "disgusting animals." And that is just a few of the names he has called women over the years.

During the Republican Presidential primary, his major critique of rival Carly Fiorina was that no one would vote for her because of "her face," and he also suggested that women should be "punished" for having an abortion.[2] He joked about "dating" he daughter. The list goes on and on. One would think that Trump is auditioning for a part in a sequel to the movie *Animal House*, not for the Presidency.

Back in the 1990s, Trump publicly humiliated his then current wife, Ivana, by appearing in public in the company of another woman, Marla Maples. While still married to Ivana, he belittled her in a *Vanity Fair* interview, saying: "I would never buy Ivana any decent jewels or pictures. Why give her negotiable assets?"[3] In 1991, he told *Esquire Magazine* that "it doesn't really matter what [they] write as long as you've got a young and beautiful piece of ass."[4]

In 2006, during his public feud with Rosy O'Donnell, Trump commented on the TV show Entertainment Tonight: "Rosie O'Donnell is disgusting, both inside and out. If you take a look at her, she's a slob. How does she even get on television? If I were running The View, I'd fire Rosie. I'd look her right in that fat, ugly face of hers and say, 'Rosie, you're fired.'" He couldn't resist adding: "We're all a little chubby but Rosie's just worse than most of us. But it's not the chubbiness — Rosie is a very unattractive person, both inside and out." Trump also went out of his way to offend the entire LGBT community by saying that "Rosie's a person who's very lucky to have a girlfriend."[5]

On March 2, 2013, Trump took another shot at O'Donnell by tweeting: "How much would it take for you to make out with Rosie O'Donnell? One trillion, at least!

The *New York Post* reported that former contestants in The Apprentice complained that Trump consistently objectified them. For example, in the fall of 2010, Mahsa Saeidi-Azcuy, a former Brooklyn prosecutor who was demoted and then quit after appearing on The Apprentice without first advising her bosses, claimed: "So much of the boardroom discussion concerned the appearance of the female contestants—discussing the female contestants' looks—who he found to be hot." Referring to Trump, she commented: "He asked the men to rate the women — he went down the line and asked the guys, 'Who's the most beautiful on the women's team?'" Another contestant, Gene Folkes, a 46-year-old financial adviser, said: "I think it was most uncomfortable when he had one [female] contestant come around the board table and twirl around."[6]

In 2011, Trump was in court testifying in a deposition over a failed Florida real estate project, when lawyer Elizabeth Beck asked to take a break to breastfeed her three-month-old daughter. Trump and his team objected, so she pulled out her breast pump to prove it. Trump's reaction was to walk out of the room, telling Beck she was 'disgusting.'[7]

Also in 2011, when New York Times columnist Gail Collins wrote about rumors that Trump was about to declare bankruptcy, Trump sent her a copy of her own article with her picture circled with a handwritten note: "The face of a dog!"

On May 11, 2012, after the singer Cher criticized Mitt Romney, Trump commented negatively about her appearance and her reputed elective surgeries: "I promise not to talk about your massive plastic surgeries that didn't work," he tweeted.

On August 28, 2012, Trump insulted *Huffington Post* editor Arianna Huffington by tweeting that she "is unattractive both inside and out. I fully understand why her former husband left her for a man – he made a good decision." On April 7, 2015, he followed up with a tweet: "How much money is the extremely unattractive (both inside and out) Arianna Huffington paying her poor ex-hubby for the use of his name?"[8]

On March 3, 2013, on Celebrity Apprentice, when former Playboy playmate Brande Roderick knelt down in front of Trump in the boardroom to ask him to name her as the next project manager, Trump made an off-color oral sex joke by saying: "It must be a pretty picture. You dropping to your knees".

Many of the complaints against Trump by women relate to the Miss USA pageant, of which he was a co-owner. While Trump cannot be seriously faulted for seeing a financial opportunity in a business featuring beautiful, scantily-clad women, he apparently went far over the line of propriety in dealing with many of these impressionable young women.

In 2009, beauty queen Carrie Prejean wrote about the 'Trump rule' in her book, referring to the Miss USA pageant, of which Trump is co-owner. She claimed that Trump had the girls parade in front of him so he could separate those he found attractive from those he didn't. As detailed in the *Telegraph* article, she wrote: "Many of the girls found this exercise humiliating. Some of the girls were sobbing backstage after [he] left, devastated to have failed even before the competition really began ... it was as though we had been stripped bare."[9]

According to reporting by Matt Viser of *The Boston Globe*, Trump apparently got into the pageant business in 1992, when he met with George Houraney and Jill Harth, a couple that ran the American Dream Pageant. Harth alleges Trump groped her at a party after telling her to bring some models with her. In a limo afterward, another model said she heard him say that "all women are bimbos" and most "gold diggers."[10] As reported in an article in *The Atlantic*, Trump reportedly joined another model in bed, uninvited, late at night. On other occasions, he forced Harth into bedrooms and made passes at her, she said. Harth sued Trump, alleging sexual misbehavior, while the couple together sued him for breach of contract. She also claimed that Trump had kept black women out of the pageant.[11]

A few years later, Trump bought the Miss Universe pageant, which also includes Miss USA and Miss Teen USA. "Honestly, when I bought [Miss Universe], the bathing suits got smaller, and the heels got higher, and the ratings went up," he told *Vanity Fair*. By 2015, he operated Miss Universe as a joint venture with NBC, but after he defamed Mexican immigrants at his campaign launch, Univision, and NBC both announced they would not air the pageant. Trump bought out NBC's share, then promptly sold the company.

On August 8, 2015, after the first Republican debate where Megyn Kelly gave Trump a rough time over allegations regarding his sexism, he proved her point by calling her a "bimbo" on Twitter. In a later CNN interview, he suggested her questioning was a result of her menstruating: "You could see there was blood coming out of her eyes. Blood coming out of her wherever." [12]

On August 16, 2015, Trump told the *New York Times* during an interview, referring to the German supermodel: "Heidi Klum. Sadly, she's no longer a 10." In response, Klum posted a video on Twitter in which she wore a t-shirt with '10' written on it.

On March 30, 2016, during an MSNBC interview, Trump call for "some form of punishment" for women who have abortions. When it was clear that he was facing a huge blow-back on this position, Trump reversed himself two hours later, saying that he would punish doctors who performed abortions, but not the women themselves.

Trump has explained that his thinking on abortion had "evolved" since he started campaigning for the Republican nomination. He takes the position that *Roe v. Wade*, 410 U.S. 113 (1973), the Supreme Court ruling legalizing abortion, should be overturned and that individual states should be allowed to ban it. According to his campaign, Trump now believes abortion should be legal only in instances of rape, incest or when the life of the mother is at stake. In fact, he said that he would be willing to shut down the US Government to defund Planned Parenthood.

On May 8, 2016, in response to Hillary Clinton's outspoken criticism of Trump on women's issues, Trump accused her of being an 'enabler" of her husband's affairs by destroying the lives of his mistresses. At a rally, he said: "Bill Clinton was the worst in history, and I have to listen to her talking about it?" he said in Eugene, Oregon. "Just remember this: She was an unbelievably nasty, mean enabler. "And what she did to a lot of those women is disgraceful. So put that in her bonnet and let's see what happens."

But Trump's sexism extends far beyond the personal attacks and the objectification of women. He also has a checkered record on economic issues that are critically important to most women, such as the equal pay issue. On June 4, 2016, the *Boston Globe* reported that men working for Donald Trump's presidential campaign made, on average, about 35 percent more than women working on the campaign. In contrast, the *Globe* found that Hillary Clinton's campaign paid men and women equally.[13]

Trump has also taken a very cavalier attitude towards the problem of sexual assaults in the military. On May 7, 2013, Trump blamed the high number of sex assaults in the military to the fact that the military put men and women together as if it was inevitable that many women would be attacked as a result. He tweeted: "26,000 unreported sexual assaults in the military-only 238 convictions. What did these geniuses expect when they put men & women together?"[14]

It is no surprise, therefore, that Trump's blatant misogynistic record has alienated a segment of the population that comprised more than one-half the voters in America: Women. In fact, more than 70 percent of registered women voters view Trump negatively, and 47% of Republican women primary voters said that they "could not imagine" themselves supporting Trump. But as least he has locked in the misogynist voting bloc, although no polls specifically target that demographic.

7

TRUMP AND THE WALL

Central to Donald Trump's campaign for the Presidency is the promise to build a wall across the United States' southern border and to deport all 11 million undocumented immigrants now in the country. Once all undocumented immigrants are deported with the help of a "deportation task force", the "good" ones, according to Trump, will be permitted to come back legally into the country. In a CNN interview, Trump explained: "I want to move them out, and we're going to move them back in and let them be legal, but they have to be in here legally." There would be no exceptions, even for the so-called "Dreamers", *i.e.*, those young undocumented immigrants who were brought to this country by their parents as children and are now afforded limited protection from deportation, but still don't have a "path to citizenship."[1]

In a report by *BuzzFeed* during the Republican primary season, Trump told the *New York Times* in off-the-record talks, that his public statements about deporting all illegal aliens was just bluster and a starting point for negotiations, saying he might not actually deport the undocumented immigrants. Trump, however, refused a request that he release the transcript of his *New York Times* interviews. He later objected to the characterization of his policy as one of "mass deportations."

After the Brussels attacks claimed by ISIS that killed at least 28 and injured more than 270, Trump told *Fox News* that "I'd close up our borders to people until we figure out what is going on."

The Wall and the Environment

In addition to the tremendous cost of such a project, a wall on the US-Mexican border would create an environmental disaster of staggering proportions. According to many environmentalists and ecologists, a wall stretched across the entire southwestern United States would impair the migratory patterns and destroy habitats and many of the fragile ecosystems in that part of the country. "The southwestern US and northwestern Mexico share their weather, rivers and wildlife," Sergio Avila-Villegas, a conservation scientist at the Arizona-Sonora Desert Museum in Tucson, told *Nature*. "The infrastructure on the border cuts through all that and divides a shared landscape in two."[2] As he further explained, the area is home to a wide diversity of species, including some that are endangered and need access to both nations to survive. In fact, the continued survival of many species depends on the freedom of movement between Mexico and the United States, and a large wall could hamper that movement.

If a wall were actually built based on Mr. Trump's current specifications, which would be at least 50 feet high and constructed out of precast concrete, the height of the wall alone could impact the movement of birds that either do not fly, such as roadrunners, or who fly low, such as pygmy owls.[3] Other species, such as bighorn sheep, that travel in small groups and rely on cross-border connections to survive, would be cut off from other members of their species on the other side of the border. Most animals migrate either to travel to breeding grounds or to seek better conditions. These cross-border migratory patterns would be cut off by the construction of a wall.

Clinton Epps, a wildlife biologist at Oregon State University in Corvallis, was one of the authors of a 2009 study published in *Conservation Biology* that suggested that a barrier would hurt the pygmy owls and bighorn sheep. He also highlighted in *Nature* the problems black bears, jaguars, and ocelots will have in the event of a border wall. Black bears in the US are particularly in danger if they cannot connect with Mexican bears.[4]

A border wall could also cut off access to food and water sources. In a 2011 interview with *Mother Nature Network*, conservation photographer Krista Schlyer found that even an existing broken-down barbed-wire fence near the border was impeding the access of animals to the area to food and water. A rancher on the Mexican side of the border said that bison from the U.S. side visited a pond on his land almost every day because it was the only year-round water source anywhere in the area. Also, a rancher on the American side of the border reported that the bison came to a particular pasture on his land, where there was a special kind of native grass."[5]

A study published by the University of Texas at Austin in 2011 identified at least 27 species that were at risk due to the existing border wall. In 2006, President George W. Bust authorized the construction of a barrier that spanned about 1,100 kilometers (around 683 miles). Similarly, it was reported by researchers that at least 27 species in a particular area along coastal California were at risk due to the existing border wall on the Mexican-US border. For example, mountain lions were spotted trying to climb over the bars.

TRUMP AND THE WALL

At a town-hall-style event on August 24, 2016, which was broadcast on *Fox News*, Trump appeared to moderate his hard-line position on undocumented immigrants in this country by suggesting that he was open to letting some of these 11 million people remain in the country if they paid "back taxes."

"No citizenship," Mr. Trump said. "They'll pay back taxes. They have to pay taxes," he added. There's no amnesty, but we will work with them." Trump added that while his supporters wanted to get the bad on out," he also had heard from less hard-line voters. They've said, "Mr. Trump, I love you, but to take a person that has been here for 15 or 20 years and throw them and the family out, it's so tough, Mr. Trump, he said."[6]

As the *New York Times* reported the next day, on August 26, 2016, Trump's trial balloon as to a possible shift of position was very similar to the positions taken by former Gov. Jeb Bush and Senator Marco Rubio, who Trump had lambasted as "soft on immigration" during the Republican primaries.

The comments, made at a town hall style event broadcast the night before on *Fox News*, were strikingly similar to the views of former Gov. Jeb Bush and Senator Marco Rubio of Florida, fellow Republicans whom Mr. Trump defeated in the primaries with charges that they were soft on immigration.[7]

Trump's signal that he was willing to soften his immigration policy was undoubtedly in response to polling showing that moderate

Republicans and independent voters were queasy about Trump's hand line position on Hispanics and others who had been in this country for decades but were still undocumented.

The flip side of the equation, however, was that Trump risked alienating his far right and conservative base. According to conservative commentators at least, the far right is inalterably opposed to any immigration policy that would permit illegal aliens to stay in the U.S. After all, his characterization of illegal Mexicans and murders and rapists has been one of the cornerstones of "Trumpism" since he first announced his candidacy.

Conservative author and commentator Ann Coulter was reported by the New York Times as being 'almost apoplectic." In her recent book entitled "*In Trump We Trust*," Ms. Coulter write that the only unforgivable sin Mr. Trump could commit would be to shift on immigration.[8]

A Trump spokeswoman, Katrina Pierson, insisted on CNN that Mr. Trump was merely changing the "words" he was using, not the proposals themselves. So the bottom line on Trump's immigration policy still seems to be (1) deport every undocumented person in the country, using a massive 'deportation force"; (2) build a wall to keep anyone from crossing the border without proper papers."

Trump's apparently was less of a stickler about the immigration laws, however, when it came to importing young, beautiful models from abroad for fun and profit. As *Mother Jones* reported on August 30, 2016, models with Trump's modeling agency were forced to work illegally in the United States, often under "sweatshop conditions", and told to lie about their immigration status[9] This report came weeks after *Politico* questioned the visa status of Trump's wife, Melania, at the time of her early modeling work in the United States.

According to the *Mother Jones* report, at least three non-citizen Trump models were employed by the agency without proper work visas. Two of these models said they were encouraged by Trump Model Management to purposely deceive U.S. Customs officials about why they were visiting the United States and to lie about where they intended to stay. In an interview, Canadian-born model Rachel Blais was quoted as saying that Trump's agency is "the most crooked company I've ever worked for, and I've worked for quite a few." [10]

Ms. Blais spent nearly three years working for Trump Model Management ("TMM"). After first signing with the agency in March 2004, she said, she performed a series of modeling jobs for Trump's company in the United States without a work visa. At *Mother Jones'* request, Blais provided a detailed financial statement from TMM and a letter from an immigration lawyer who, in the fall of 2004, eventually secured a visa that would permit her to work legally in the United States. These records show a six-month gap between when she began working in the United States for TMM and when she was granted a work visa.[11]

Two other former Trump models confirmed that TMM never obtained work permits for them while they were working on modeling assignments in the U.S. Several others who were interviewed also recalled being forced into cramped, overcrowded housing conditions and the company's insistence on charging them high rent for such less-than-luxurious accommodations. "It is like modern-day slavery," Blais added.

Mother Jones reported that a fourth model interviewed, Alexia Palmer, also "worked in the United States without a work visa after being recruited by Trump's agency from her native Jamaica."[12]

The foreign models were also apparently told to lie to federal authorities and to falsely fill out customs forms about the nature of their visits to the U.S. and where they would be living. One model, using the name "Anna" to protect her identity, said she received an explicit instruction from a Trump agency representative: "If they ask you any questions, you're just here for meetings." Anna explained her apprehension: "I was pretty on edge most of the time I was there," said Anna, about working for Trump's agency without a work visa in 2009. "I was there illegally," she said. "A sitting duck."[13]

Another former Trump model, using the name "Kate", commented to *Mother Jones*: "He doesn't want to let anyone into the US anymore." She added: "Meanwhile, behind everyone's back, he's bringing in all of these girls from all over the world, and they're working illegally."

TMM did not respond to *Mother Jones* when it requested a comment. Hope Hicks, the Trump campaign's spokesperson "declined to answer questions about Trump Model Management's use of foreign labor", saying, "That has nothing to do with me or the campaign."

Over the years, Trump used illegal immigrants for other business projects as well. As reported by *PolitiFact* in February 2016, a Trump contractor hired undocumented Polish workers sometime between 1979 and 1980 to demolish the Bonwit Teller building to make way for the construction of Trump Tower. These 200 Polish workers were known as "the Polish brigade." The Polish employees were off-the-books, working 12-hour shifts seven days a week for $4 to $5 an hour, with no overtime. Some workers were never paid what they were owed.[14]

Several years later, the local union apparently sued Trump and his business associates for allegedly cheating it out of welfare and pension contributions by hiring the undocumented immigrants. Trump blamed the contractor and denied knowing anything about the immigration status of the Polish workers, but a New York judge ruled for the union and ordering that Trump pay $325,000 plus interest. Trump appealed that ruling, but before the case could be retried, quietly agreed to settle it out of court.[15]

Also, as the *New York Times* reported in February 2016, according to federal records, Trump hired foreign guest workers at his Mar-a-Lago Club in Palm Beach, Florida, instead of using American workers. Of the nearly 300 United States residents who had applied or been referred for jobs as waiters, waitresses, cooks and housekeepers at the Club, only 17 were hired. In most cases, Mar-a-Lago sought to fill the jobs with hundreds of foreign guest workers from Romania and other countries. Trump apparently also pursued more than 500 visas for foreign workers at the Club since 2010, according to the United States

Department of Labor, while hundreds of domestic applicants failed to get the same jobs.[16]

According to the *Times* article, to get the necessary visas, Trump's Club told the U.S. government that, for the vast majority of the cases, it was simply unable to fill the openings with American workers. However, CNN reported that the Club did only the bare minimum required by law to advertise the available positions to Americans in the first place.[17]

Trump also seems to have no qualms about using undocumented workers to build his new $200 million luxury hotel in Washington, D. C., which is at the Old Post Office Pavilion site, a mere five blocks from the White House on Pennsylvania Avenue. According to a *Washington Post* article published in July 2015, these workers came primarily from Mexico, El Salvador, Honduras, and Guatemala. A Trump spokesperson blamed the use of undocumented workers as the problem of the contractor – Lend Lease – not Trump himself.

Thus, not only is Trump's plan to build a Wall, deport millions, ban Muslims and tighten immigration restrictions absurd and unworkable; it is also hypocritical since he has looked the other way and actively induced his foreign employees to break the immigration laws whenever it suited his interests.

Wednesday, August 31, 2016, was a big day for Trump and his immigration policy. On short notice, he flew into Mexico City on short notice to meet with Mexican President Enrique Pena Nieto, who has

TRUMP AND THE WALL

compared Trump to Adolph Hitler. The two met briefly before a joint press conference. Although there were no reporters present during their private meeting, Pena Nieto tweeted that he told Trump, at the outset of their conversation, that Mexico wouldn't be paying for the Wall. This directly contradicted one of Trump's comments at the press conference, when he was asked by reporters if he discussed with President Pena Nieto about whether Mexico would pay for the wall he's been talking about on the campaign trail. Trump responded: "We didn't discuss that …We discussed the wall; we didn't discuss payment of the wall."

Very odd! Both versions of reality cannot be true. One of them must be lying. I suspect that it is Trump. His entire demeanor during the press conference in Mexico City was that he wanted to avoid any confrontation with the President at all costs, and couldn't bring himself to tell the Mexican President or the Mexican people to their face while standing on Mexican soil that they were going to pay billions to build a wall they detested, whether they liked it or not. You don't accept a man's invitation to a party at his house and then insult him in front of his guests.

In other words, it is highly unlikely that Trump would be able to claim that Pena Nieto and most of his people are moral degenerates, horse thieves, murderers, rapists, and worse, and then expect to be able to walk out without some sort of donnybrook ensuing. Better to convey the message after you have said your "goodbyes" and returned home to the safety of your own house. Then you can send him any sort of nasty message or email with impunity. This was no doubt Donald Trump's thinking. He kept his mouth shut about the wall and who was going to pay for it, and when the Mexican President told him that Mexico would not pay for a wall, he just smiled and changed the subject. "I just love Mexicans," you can hear him saying. "Some of my best friends are Mexicans." "Great people, no, I really mean it. Wonderful people! Did I tell you we had a special on taco bowls on Cinco de Mayo?"

Both Trump and President Pena Nieto were very deferential during their public meetings, with both of them talking about the rights of both countries to secure their borders. It was almost surreal. Trump had been hurling insults at the Mexican people in general and their leaders in particular for months. He graphically described how Mexico was getting rid of its murderers and rapists by sending them north across the border, and then when he got face to face with the leader of this evil empire to the South, all he could muster were nice platitudes about how great the Mexican people were and how some of his best friends were Mexican.

Trump had a prime- time opportunity to point a (tiny) finger at the Mexican President and demand that Mexico pay for the wall keeping all those murderers and rapists on their side of the border, and he completely choked! He didn't even demand payment for the wall or tell the Mexican President that he had better start building massive tent cities along the border for the 11 million undocumented Mexican immigrants in the U.S. who would be soon transported by bus to the border and dropped over the wall.

Trump acted like the school bully who spends the day bragging about how he is going to beat up another student in the schoolyard after school, but when the school bell rings and the school empties out, the bully slinks past the other student without so much as a word.

All day the airwaves were filled with speculation by Trump surrogates, many of them Hispanic, touting Trump's speech later that evening in Phoenix. They said it was a major policy address on immigration that would resolve all of the conflicting signals coming from the Trump camp in recent weeks about a "softening" in Trump's immigration policy. They suggested that perhaps a more compassionate approach that recognized the countless human indignities and needless hardship that would be imposed on the 11 million Mexicans and other Latinos/Latinas who would be rounded up by the Gestapo-like deportation force that Trump was calling for. The anticipation and expectation of a new, more diplomatic, presidential and compassionate Trump was almost palpable. Surely he couldn't have been entirely serious about his plan to build a real wall along the entire border and to deport 11 million people in one fell swoop. This was just rhetoric, right? Now he was going to "pivot towards the center" and convince those moderate and undecided voters he needed to win the election that he was capable of coming up with a rational immigration policy. Right? Those rumors about him finally experiencing a crisis of conscience would be proven to be true, after his hardened heart had finally softened tales of woe from Hispanic supporters about the unfathomable pain and suffering that would be caused if longtime undocumented residents in this country were torn from their families and forcibly shipped back to Mexico.

Alas, the anticipation and the rumors were too good to be true. As soon as the "diplomatic" Trump on display in Mexico City landed in Phoenix, the old blustering bully returned as he addressed his die-hard core supporters at the mass rally waiting for him. Trump had this message for anyone who thought he was backing off his threat of mass deportation: "Anyone who has entered the United States illegally is subject to deportation," he said during his big immigration policy speech. They would be rounded up and deported without mercy, regardless of whether they were illegal workers or Dreamers or the parents of U.S. citizens.[18] They all would have to go. After all, they were criminals. They had broken the U.S. Immigration laws and would have to face exile.

Trump was equally clear that he would never consider "amnesty" or a "path to citizenship" for those illegally in the country. "Our message to the world will be this: You cannot obtain legal status, or become a citizen of the United States, by illegally entering our country. Can't do it."[19]

At the end of his speech Trump held open the vague hope for those undocumented immigrants who remained after his primary goals had been accomplished stating:

> "in several years, when we have accomplished all of our enforcement and deportation goals, and truly ended illegal immigration for good....then and only then will we be in a position to consider the appropriate disposition of those individuals who remain."[20]

Chuck Todd of NBC News's Meet the Press compared this statement to being "akin to telling someone you might get back together after your divorce.[21]" First the divorce, and then we will see what happens. First, we deport you and then when you are back in Mexico where you belong, we will see about letting you back into the U.S as a legal immigrant. Thanks, Donald.

Obviously, the strain on Mr. Trump of having to act "presidential" while in Mexico was too much for him. He had to revert to the old mean-spirited demagogue that we have come to loathe and, sadly, some misguided souls among us have come to love.

8

TRUMP AND THE RUSSIANS

Understanding Paul Manafort and His International Ties

At first, I was surprised when I heard that Donald Trump had hired Paul Manafort to be one of his chief advisors, and then named him as his temporary Campaign Manager. I had known Manafort from years before when he was the chief advisor to Viktor Yanukovich, the former President of Ukraine. At the time, I was representing Yulia Tymoshenko, the former Prime Minister of Ukraine, who was one of the leaders of the political opposition to Yanukovich and his pro-Russian Party of Regions, which had steered Ukraine back into the Russian orbit. Yanukovich and his cronies, including his appointees in the Ukraine Chief Prosecutor's Office, had embarked on a campaign to harass and silence Tymoshenko and other opposition leaders through a series of baseless and politically-motivated investigations and prosecutions on a variety of trumped-up charges (no pun intended). Tymoshenko and other opposition leaders were thrown into jail and arbitrarily detained under horrendous conditions. Tymoshenko was denied the urgent medical attention she required to relieve her excruciating back pain and other ailments. The U.S., the European Union and human rights groups around the world protested these incarcerations and political show-trials reminiscent of the Stalinist era.

When there was a near-universal outcry of opposition to Yanukovich's strong-arm tactics and the suppression of political and human rights, Yanukovich relied upon his old friend and advisor, Paul

Manafort, to refurbish his political image, which had never been very good. Rumors that Yanukovich had been a low-level member of a criminal organization in his hometown of Donetsk had persisted since the time he had been sentenced in 1967 to a three-year prison term for participating in a robbery and assault. In June 1970, he was convicted for a second time on charges of assault, and sentenced to two years of imprisonment. Yanukovich was also accused of having participated in the attack and rape of a young woman, which he denied.

While in prison, Yanukovich solidified his credentials with the dominant Russian-based organized crime group operating in Eastern Ukraine, and after his release, this same group provided much of the financing and muscle needed to propel young Yanukovich's administrative and political career. [1]

Manafort's History of Representing Repressive Regimes

At first blush, it would seem odd for Yanukovich to choose a political adviser such as Paul Manafort, who was based almost half way around the world in the Washington, D.C. area and didn't speak a word of Ukrainian or Russian (Yanukovich's native tongue from Eastern Ukraine). Moreover, Manafort was primarily known – at least in the U.S. -- for his rather specialized talent for managing the delegate count and floor operations at Republican Presidential conventions, starting with Gerald Ford's success in turning back the insurgent campaign of Governor Ronald Reagan in 1984.

However, what was less widely known about Manafort (but was known to Yanukovich and his associates) was that he had successfully pursued a parallel career outside the U.S. representing some of the most oppressive and autocratic leaders that other U.S. consultants wouldn't touch with a ten-foot pole. Manafort's dubious client list included President Marcos, who was eventually forced to flee the Philippines, and the despotic leaders of the Dominican Republic, Nigeria, Kenya, Equatorial Guinea, and Somalia.

Where other less-talented or less tenacious consultants had given up in frustration trying to "re-make" the public image of these strongmen, who almost uniformly had built up well-deserved reputations as sadistic torturers and human rights violators, Manafort – for a handsome price – worked hard at coaching his clients and smoothing out some of the rougher edges until they had a softer and gentler image. No detail was too unimportant. He coached them on how to hold their hands in public, how to wave to a crowd, what kind of haircut they should have, and – as more recently in the case of Donald Trump – how to use a teleprompter.

Soon there was a long line of despots from around the globe who were vying for Manafort's seemingly magical and transformational services. All of these leaders had a poor (and well-deserved) public relations problem. These men held onto the levers of power in their respective countries -- not through the vagaries of the democratic process -- but, rather, through violence, terror, the conscription of child soldiers, the sale of blood diamonds and the recreational torture and murder of political opponents.

As the *Daily Beast* reported in an article dated April 13, 2016, one of Manafort's first clients was Jonas Savimbi, who led a guerilla army battling the Angolan government during the country's brutal civil war.

Savimbi hired Manafort's lobbying firm to help him get financial support from the U.S. government for his guerilla army, UNITA (National Union for the Total Independence of Angola).

Manafort delivered big time for Savimbi. As *Time* Magazine reported in 1986: "Doors swung open all over town for the guerrilla leader, who was dapperly attired in a Nehru suit and ferried about in a stretch limousine." Then-Senate Majority Leader Bob Dole urged the State Department to send heavy arms to Savimbi's guerilla army. Savimbi retained in 1989 to orchestrate a media blitz. They got him booked on *60 Minutes* and *Nightline*, as the *Post* noted.[2]

In essence, Manafort helped repackage Savimbi as a valiant anti-communist 'freedom fighter,' as the Nairobi's *The Daily Nation* reported. According to *The Washington Post*, Manafort's firm was well-compensated for its services. Savimbi paid the firm $600,000 in 1985 alone.[3]

It is generally agreed now that, from a historical perspective, Manafort's impressive efforts on behalf of Savimbi slowed the peace process and significantly protracted the hostilities. From 1986 to 1987, the Reagan administration sent a total of $42 million to UNITA, which according to Joy James's book *Resisting State Violence: Radicalism, Gender, and Race in U.S. Culture*, Savimbi's army "maimed or killed tens of thousands, creating one of the largest amputee populations in the world through its laying of land mines in farm fields, roads, and school yards." A Human Rights Watch report described the tactics employed by the Savimbi forces as: "Indiscriminate killings, mutilation of limbs or ears, and beatings were used by rebels to punish suspected government sympathizers or as a warning against betraying UNITA." The Report further found that "UNITA continued to forcibly recruit men and teenage boys to fight. Girls were held in sexual slavery and used as a source of forced labor."[4]

Manafort's firm also represented other leaders who favored the use of torture as an everyday political tool. A 1992 report from the Center for Public Integrity listed the consulting firm of "Black, Manafort, Stone and Kelly" as one of the lobbying firms to profit the most by doing business with foreign governments that violated their people's human rights. From 1991 to 1992, Manafort's firm made $3.3 million from what the Center for Public Integrity called "the torturers' lobby."[5]

From 1990 to 1993, the Kenyan government paid Manafort's firm more than $1.4 million to lobby the U.S. government to send them more aid. This was a particularly tough sell since the U.S. was highly critical of the country's human rights record, as reported by the Center for Public Integrity. Severe police brutality, prisoner abuse, and crackdowns on hunger strikers all drew international criticism. Nevertheless, the country still collected $38.3 million in aid from the U.S. government, due in large measure to the efforts of Manafort and his partners.[6]

Mobutu Sese Seko, dictator of Zaire (now the Democratic Republic of Congo) also benefitted from Manafort's lobbying expertise. *The Guardian* described him as "one of Africa's most flamboyantly corrupt leaders."[7] Human-rights activists held Seko responsible for government-sanctioned torture, detainment, and rape. "Quantitatively, I think Zaire has the worst human rights record in Africa," one UN official told the *Chicago Tribune* in 1997. "In terms of social and economic rights and the number of state actors violating those rights, it's massive. And the bulk of human rights violations in this country never will be known. It's a black hole."[8]

This was precisely the client profile that attracted Manafort. The dictator of Zaire retained Manafort's firm in 1989 for a flat fee of $1 million a year.

In 1985, Manafort's firm was hired by the Chamber of Philippine Manufacturers, Exporters, and Tourists Associations, which had close ties with President-For-Life Ferdinand Marcos, whose regime put the country under martial law and was responsible for hundreds of cases of torture. In 2004, Transparency International listed him as one of the world's 10 most notorious leaders of the previous two decades (along with Mobutu Sese Seko, other Manafort clients).[9] They estimate Marcos embezzled between $5 million and $10 million from his people. Almost 50,000 Filipinos have filed claims for reparations for crimes against them during Marcos's era of martial law, according to the Philippine news site *Rappler.com*.

Time reported that Marcos paid the firm $900,000 to refurbish its image. However, shortly after Manafort's firm was retained, Marcos was forced to flee the country. Under a deal negotiated by Senator Paul Laxalt of Nevada and Manafort, Marcos was granted asylum in the U.S. When Marcos' plane landed in Honolulu, a customs inspection revealed a huge cache of gold bars that Marcos had withdrawn from the Philippines federal reserve bank as a going away present to himself. The gold was confiscated by U.S. authorities, but in return, Marcos and his family were issued bearer bond certificates by the U.S. Treasury, with each bearer bond representing $50 million. After that, whenever Marcos or his family needed some walking around money, they would cash in one of the certificates to finance their extravagant lifestyle.

But as Manafort learned, the gold that Marcos spirited out of the Philippines was only the tip of the iceberg. What Manafort also learned was that Marcos knew the location in the Philippines where the Yamamoto gold cache had been hidden. During the height of Japan's domination of the Far East and the Pacific during World War II, and after the fall of the Philippines and withdrawal of U.S. forces, Japanese General Yamamoto had most of the gold bullion that had been seized from the British colonies that had fallen transferred to the Philippines. After the end of the war and the rise of Marcos' political fortunes, Marcos invited the surviving Japanese officers who had supervised the burying of the gold back to the Philippines as his personal guest. After they had been appropriately entertained for a few weeks in Manila, they revealed the location of the gold to Marcos, who confirmed this information by having the retired officers bring him to the site of the gold itself. Marcos then had one of his closest and trusted associates execute the officers on the spot and disposed of the bodies. Marcos did not reveal the location of the gold to Manafort or anyone else, but he bragged that it was worth at least $50 billion.

Another dictator who both made Transparency International's list and Paul Manafort's was Sani Abacha of Nigeria. He hired Manafort's firm in 1998 as part of "an aggressive public relations and lobbying campaign to persuade Americans that he was the leader of a progressive emerging democracy," according to *The New York Times*.[10] This was another client who presented huge problems for Manafort since a 1997 State Department report detailed persistent torture and abuse under the Abacha regime. [D]etainees frequently died while in custody," reads the report, "and there were credible reports that security officers seeking to extract confessions regularly beat suspects, detainees, and convicted prisoners. Security guards also routinely tortured prisoners with whippings, suspension by the limbs from the ceiling, burning with candles, and extraction of teeth.

Manafort's "Make-Over" of Ukraine's Pro-Russian President

Just as he had done for numerous other despots, Manafort used all of his considerable skills in his make-over of Yanukovich. Where others derided Manafort's efforts to re-make Yanukovich as a hopeless attempt to put "lipstick on a pig," Manafort molded this rough-hewn apparatchik -- who could easily have been mistaken as having all the charm as a hitman for the Russian mob -- into a cosmopolitan contemporary-looking statesman. Yanukovich started sporting a more European-looking hair style (rather than the 1950's Politburo Stalinist look he had favored), waved for the cameras with a Western-style ease, and even started responding to the long-suffering Ukrainian crowds by saying, "I can feel your pain" (a Manafort-favorite saying).

Meanwhile, under Manafort's tutelage, the Yanukovich regime ratcheted up its anti-Western European rhetoric as part of a campaign to prevent Ukraine from pursuing membership in the European Union. As part of the age-old effective strategy of "divide and conquer," Yanukovich started pandering to the worst fears of the Russian-speaking minority in the industrialized Eastern Ukraine, spreading totally fabricated rumors that any alliance with the EU would lead to the persecution of the Russian-speaking minorities. Also, when NATO held some naval exercises in the Mediterranean near Crimea, Yanukovich followed Manafort's advice to denounce these exercises as an infringement on Ukrainian sovereignty and as part of a European plot to force Ukraine to join the EU.

American Ambassador William Taylor told Manafort at a meeting in the U.S. Embassy in Kiev in 2006 that it was against U.S. interests for Manafort and Yanukovich to be steering Ukraine towards Russia and away from Europe and the West.[11][12] Manafort just ignored him and continued to advise the Ukrainian pro-Russian political forces to do everything in their power to keep Ukraine out of the EU and NATO. All other appeals to Manafort's patriotism by U.S. officials were equally rebuffed, and Manafort continued to be the primary Western spokesperson and apologist for Yanukovich and his pro-Russian allies in Ukraine.

Manafort and Gates Violate U.S. Laws Requiring That They Register As Agents of a Foreign Government

On August 15, 2016, the *New York Times* reported that a secret handwritten ledger maintained by the Yanukovich Administration in Kiev, Ukraine listed Manafort as the intended recipient of $12.7 million in "off the books" and undisclosed cash payments from 2007 to 2012. The money was from Yanukovich's pro-Russian political party for his work on behalf of this pro-Russian autocrat, who was deposed during a popular uprising in February 2014.[13] Government investigators in Ukraine describe the ledger as evidence of a corrupt network to loot

Ukrainian assets and to influence elections during the period of time when Manafort was a chief adviser to Viktor Yanukovich.

These secret Ukrainian ledgers also apparently contained information regarding an $18 million deal to sell Ukrainian cable TV assets to a partnership organized by Manafort and Oleg Deripaska, a Russian oligarch and a close ally of President Putin. [14]

Two days later, on August 17, 2016, the *Associated Press* reported that Manafort and Rick Gates, his Manafort's then-deputy in the Trump campaign organization, helped Yanukovich's pro-Russian governing party in Ukraine to secretly route at least $2.2 million in payments to two prominent Washington lobbying firms in 2012 for the purpose of influencing U.S. policy towards the Yanukovich regime. During the period when Manafort and Gates were consultants to the Ukraine president's political party, the Party of Regions, they helped steer money from a pro-Yanukovych nonprofit, the European Centre for a Modern Ukraine, to these two Washington lobbying firms, Podesta Group Inc. and Mercury LLC. [15]

By moving the Yanukovich party's money through this ostensibly nonprofit organization to the U.S. lobbying firms, Manafort and Gates concocted a scheme to disguise the real source of the funds, which all originated with the pro-Russian Ukraine government. Manafort and Gates wanted to structure the transaction in such a way that it would appear that a foreign government was trying to influence U.S. policy, especially since the U.S. policy and American interests at the time favored a Ukraine government that was more closely aligned with Western interests rather than those of Russia. The European Centre assisted this illegal scheme in making it appear that the lobbying effort was not being conducted by a foreign power by providing false public assurances that none of its activities was directly or indirectly supervised, directed, controlled, financed or subsidized by Ukraine's government or any of the country's political parties.[16]

After being introduced by Manafort and Gates to the lobbying firms, the European nonprofit paid the Podesta Group $1.13 million between June 2012 and April 2014 to lobby Congress, the White House National Security Council, the State Department and other federal agencies, according to U.S. lobbying records.

The nonprofit also paid $1.07 million over roughly the same period to Mercury to lobby Congress. Among other things, these lobbyists used their considerable political influence in Washington to defeat an effort to have the U.S. Congress pass a resolution condemning the pro-Russian Yanukovich government for its imprisonment of former Prime Minister Tymoshenko and other human rights violations.

Both the direct $12.7 million in cash payments to Manafort by Yanukovich's pro-Russian political party, and the scheme to route $2.2 million in lobbying money from Ukraine to the Washington lobbyists, violated the U.S. Foreign Agents Registration Act (FARA). FARA is a U.S. law requiring all U.S. lobbyists representing foreign leaders or their political parties to provide the U.S. Department of Justice with detailed reports regarding their actions. FARA requires those who register as lobbyists on behalf of foreign governments or parties to detail the home addresses of lobbyists and descriptions of all receipts, payments, political contributions and details about any lectures, emails, pamphlets or press releases they create.

A violation of FARA is a felony criminal offense, and can result in up to five years in prison and a fine of up to $250,000. This law, generally known as the foreign agent law, is enforced by a relatively small division within the counter-espionage section of the Justice Department's National Security Division.

Manafort Sets Up A Money Laundering Scheme With A Ukrainian Oligarch

During the many years that Manafort worked in Ukraine, Yanukovich and the Ukrainian oligarchs who surrounded him opened up a whole new world of opulence to Manafort, complete with palaces, solid gold golf clubs, a private lake with a replica of a Spanish galleon for entertainment, and pet ostriches wandering around the Versailles-style gardens surrounding the Presidential Palace just outside Kiev. Yanukovich had a customized private helicopter built that was bigger and much more expensive than any used by a U.S. President, which Yanukovich never tired of reminding Manafort and others in his inner circle.

One of the wealthiest and most powerful Ukrainian oligarchs that Manafort was introduced to was Dymitri Firtash, who was one of Yanukovich's primary financial backers and a close associate of Putin. Firtash had literally made billions of dollars through a very simple yet effective scheme engineered with Putin and his associates who managed Gazprom, the Russian-owned natural gas company. Gazprom sold significant amounts of natural gas to Firtash's company, RUE, who then marked up the price and resold the gas to Ukraine and Western Europe. RUE served no legitimate service to justify this markup in price, and never actually took possession of the natural gas. In other words, this was a pure "skimming" operation, the sole purpose of which was to divert billions of dollars to Firtash and RUE, who then doled out generous kickbacks and payoffs to Putin and his cronies in Russia, and Yanukovich and his pro-Russian allies in Ukraine. This was the grease that kept the corrupt regimes of Yanukovich and Putin chugging along year after year.

The most difficult part of the scheme was not where the money would be coming from. The source of the funds was from RUE's markup of the billions of dollars in natural gas sales from Russia (actually mostly from Turkmenistan) to Ukraine and the West. The tricky part of the equation was to disguise the distribution of those ill-gotten gains back to Putin in Russia and Yanukovich in Ukraine. The distribution route for the money had to be intentionally made so complicated and circuitous that it would be impossibly difficult to trace. This is called money laundering: the dirty money goes in, and the "clean" untraceable money comes out.

Putin and Yanukovich and their cronies were always looking for new ways to launder the tidal wave of cash being generated by Firtash's gas trading activities. Manafort opened up an entirely new world of money laundering opportunities for Firtash by inviting him to "invest" in real estate deals in New York and elsewhere in North America and the Caribbean. Firtash and Manafort were soon in business together.

With a commitment of an initial $25 million from Firtash, Manafort formed CMZ Ventures in New York with an office located on the 20th floor of 1501 Broadway in Manhattan. In addition to Manafort (the "M" in CMZ), the two other name partners in the Company were Brad Zackson, a real estate broker with the Donald Trump organization, and Arthur Cohen, a longstanding real estate developer in the New York area. Firtash was the "silent partner" in the Company and the source of the funding. Manafort also knew (or should have known) that by teaming up with Firtash, he was also doing business with Firtash's primary backer, Seymeon Mogalevich, the godfather of Russian organized crime.

Manafort had made a successful career of dealing with shady characters, so he teamed up with Firtash and Mogalevich with nary a qualm. Manafort made it clear to his other U.S. partners and to Company employees that he was to be the only contact person for Firtash, and he flew off to Monaco and other European locations to meet with Firtash.

In addition to wiring $25 million to New York in 2008, Manafort also secured a commitment from Firtash to provide the financing for a $100 million investment fund, with Manafort and his U.S. partners receiving a $1.5 million fee for supposedly managing the money. In one email dated June 8, 2009, which was publicly disclosed in the U.S. lawsuit brought by Tymoshenko and others in the United States District Court for the Southern District of New York, Manafort informed one of his partners, Brad Zackson: "Basically, DF [Dimitri Firtash] is still totally on board, and a wire will be forthcoming either the end of this week or next week as a partial payment on the 1.5 [million in fees to Manafort and his U.S. partners].

To successfully disguise CMZ Ventures as a legitimate real estate company, the Company entered into an options contract to purchase the

Drake Hotel site in midtown Manhattan, and drew up plans to build a new luxury commercial and residential tower to be called "Bulgari Towers."

During 2008, CMZ also hired some young, bright employees who were looking to gain some experience in the real estate development field. Among those they hired were Scott Snizek and Christy Rullis, both of whom I later represented after CMZ failed to pay them any salary and even denied that they were employees when they filed for unemployment benefits.

In fact, Scott, Christy and the rest of the employees were never actually paid any salary at all. Instead, they were periodically given "expense" checks as reimbursement for fictitious expenses that they had incurred. The apparent reason for this was that the Company did not want to go through the trouble of establishing a legitimate payroll system, with tax withholding and other bothersome requirements, because it never intended to stay in business for very long. The primary purpose was to launder sufficient funds for Firtash through a labyrinth of bank accounts and an alphabet soup of sub-companies, with Manafort, Zackson, and Cohen receiving sizable cuts along the way for their money-laundering purposes.

Christy Rullis recalled being extremely puzzled as to why she was being asked to open bank accounts in Panama and other Caribbean locations when the projects that they were supposedly financing, such as the Drake Hotel project, were located in New York. It wasn't until much later after the Company abruptly closed its doors in January 2009 without actually ever closing on any project, that it had never been the partners' intention to operate a legitimate real estate company.

Scott, Christy and some of the other employees applied for unemployment insurance payments, but could not produce any pay stubs or other evidence that they had actually been employees at the Company. This had been particularly hard on Christy Rullis since she had just renewed her apartment lease in Manhattan, thinking that she would have a steady income over the next year or so, only to have the rug abruptly pulled out from under her.

It was only after several weeks of investigation by the New York State Labor Department and various unemployment insurance hearings that Scott, Christy and some of the other employees in the Company were able to establish that they had in fact been actual employees of the Company. They were then able to start receiving some unemployment insurance benefits.

However, perhaps most damaging to Scott and Christy were the damage to their careers. The Company had been "sold" to them by Manafort and Zackson as an excellent opportunity for them to get valuable experience in the real estate development field, and it appeared – at least on the surface – that the Company was working on legitimate real estate projects. In addition to the Drake Hotel project, the Company was developing plans to build a major resort on a small deserted island in the Bahamas, and Scott actually spent some of his own money traveling down to the potential site to do some preliminary investigation. However, this real estate project also evaporated into thin air, once Manafort, Firtash, and Zackson had accomplished their primary role. The plan was to launder millions of dollars of Firtash's money through seemingly legitimate business enterprises, and then abruptly closing down the "front" business (CMZ) without having actually "closed" on any of the real estate deals. Along the way, Manafort and Zackson were well compensated for their troubles.

Made For Each Other: Manafort Teams Up With Trump

Most political campaigns carefully "vet" their chief advisors to make sure that there is nothing about their past that will embarrass the candidate. I obviously am not privy as to what extent (if at all) Trump was aware of Manafort's international consulting background before he signed him up as a principal adviser, and then campaign manager. However, if he did know about Manafort's extensive work on behalf of Yanukovich, and that Manafort was a major architect of Yankovich's blatantly anti-American and pro-Russian policies, it apparently made no difference to Trump, who was already crafting a foreign policy position that tilted steeply in favor of Russia.

Manafort and Trump had much in common when it came to Russia. Both Manafort and Trump shared an admiration for Vladimir Putin, who assumed the traditional role as the Russian strongman, tamping down on any real moves towards democracy, free speech, and respect for fundamental human rights in Russia.

Manafort and Trump also shared the entrepreneur's instinct for wanting to gain access to the Russian capital, which had largely stagnated due to the EU and U.S. sanctions against Russian for its repeated violations of human rights and aggression towards neighboring countries, including Ukraine. Trump got a taste of "From Russian With Love" at the Miss Universe pageant held in Russian, where he was suitable impressed even though Putin never even stopped by to say "hello."

Manafort's relationship with Putin and Russia run much deeper than Trump's. When Manafort was masterminding Yanukovich's anti-U.S. policy in Ukraine, he established a relationship with Oleg Deripaska –a Russian oligarch with close ties to Putin. I happened to learn of Manafort's business relationship with Deripaska after the Ukrainian people decided that they had had enough of Yanukovich's corruption and excesses, and his unabashed intention to turn Ukraine back into a Russian vassal state.

Peaceful student demonstrations at Independence Square (EuroMaidan) in downtown Kiev were met with violent suppression by Yanukovich, who ordered military sharpshooters to pick off leaders from the surrounding buildings. Finally, Yanukovich and his cronies were forced to flee Kiev, leaving behind thousands of incriminating documents that they did not have time enough to dispose of. The sauna of the General Prosecutor's mansion was filled with papers, one of which was a memo sent by Rick Gates, Manafort's right-hand man in the Trump campaign organization, to two of Deripaska's associates, discussing a possible business investment by Deripaska.

We eventually learned that Deripaska did, in fact, invest millions of dollars in a Manafort-controlled company, Pericles LLC, that was supposed to invest in various real estate projects in the U.S. and the Caribbean but never did so. The money just "disappeared" according to court papers later filed by Deripaska's lawyers, and for a period of time, Manafort also went "missing." Strange happenings for an "America First" Presidential campaign manager, who willingly climbed into bed with both the autocratic leaders of Russia and Ukraine, as well as their oligarchs. Manafort knew full well that the political and economic leaders of both countries, at least under the Yanukovich and Putin regimes, were little more than criminal organizations holding tenaciously onto their power through systematic terror, intimidation, extortion and endemic corruption.

Manafort's Huge Financial Windfall from His Russian and Ukrainian Clients

Based on the information that has come to light to date, there is approximate $64.05 million in unexplained payment to Manafort, either directly or through entities that he controls, relating to either illegal payments received from the Yanukovich Administration or suspicious real estate transaction involving Deripaska and Firtash.

According to the anti-corruption investigators in Ukraine, there are handwritten entries on a secret ledger showing 22 payments totaling $12.8 million that was earmarked for Manafort. Also, Russian oligarch Deripaska invested $18.90 million with Pericles, ostensibly for the Black Sea Cable telecom purchase, plus a fee of $7.35 million, for a total of $26.25 million. Added to this was the $25 million that Manafort and ZMC Investors received from Ukrainian oligarch Firtash (through his DF Group), ostensibly for the Drake Hotel deal in Manhattan that never closed, with the disposition of this $25 million never accounted for. [17]

Manafort's Real Estate Holdings and Financial Sleight of Hand

Much of the small fortune that Manafort amassed as a result of his Russian and Ukrainian connections was used to purchase real estate. The most prominent of these purchases was Manafort's apartment at Trump Tower (#43G). He also bought another apartment in the Soho section of Manhattan, at 27-29 Howard Street, Unit 4. He originally bought these apartments through shell companies, John Hannah LLC and MC Soho Holdings, but it appears that he later transferred these into his own name. Manafort also owns houses on Long Island at 174 Jobs Lane in Bridgehampton, New York, and another at 10 St. James Drive, Palm Beach Gardens, Florida 33418. Manafort and his wife purchased the Florida property from John Hannah LLC on January 27, 2015, for zero consideration, but then, on April 7, 2015, they took out a $3 million mortgage on the property. The purpose of taking his Florida property out of the LLC and putting it in his personal name and that of his wife appears to be so that he can benefit from Florida's generous Homestead Exemption, which protects a Florida resident's property from creditors.

Manafort Exits the Trump Campaign, But His Spirit Lives On

After a series of news articles in mid-August 2016 had disclosed further details regarding the extent of his ties with the pro-Russian Yanukovich Administration and the millions that he had allegedly received in "off-the-books" cash payment, Manafort's role in the Trump campaign was quickly downgraded. He was finally cut loose entirely from the campaign. His faithful deputy, Rick Gates, stayed on, no doubt to maintain the close working relationship between the Trump campaign and the pro-Putin forces in Russia and Ukraine. Before Manafort left, however, he sharply disputed the allegations, adding that he had completely cut his ties with Ukraine politics in 2014. Even this proved to be a lie.

The *Washington Post* article on Manafort that appeared on August 18, 2016 disclosed that Manafort continued to work for the Party of Regions, now called the Opposition Bloc, even after Yanukovich was forced to flee Kiev in February 2014. He was seen in Ukraine during 2015, and it was reported that he was there to negotiate for money he was owed for consulting with this new pro-Russian party. The *Post* further reported that Ukrainian business registration records showed that Manafort did not close his business in Kiev until April 2016, which was one month after he joined the Trump campaign. [18]

Indeed, Trump and Manafort were made for each other, and even though Manafort does not continue to hold any official position in the Trump campaign, his pro-Russian and corrupting influence undoubtedly continues to leave an indelible mark on Trump's Presidential bid. God help America.

Trump and Putin: Made For Each Other

For many months, Trump publicly bragged about his close relationship with Russian President Vladimir Putin, even claiming that Putin had referred to him as "a genius," despite the fact that there is no record of Putin ever making that comment and, indeed, no record of the two ever meeting.

In November 2015, Trump said during a TV interview of Putin, "I got to know him very well," referring to his numerous trips to Moscow over the years, especially the extended stay there during the Miss Universe Pageant.

Then Trump started refusing to answer questions as to whether he had actually met Putin or not, undoubtedly linked to the fact that he began taking some significant heat from the press over his continual boasts about his close relationship with Putin. He stopped describing his relationship with Putin as a mutual admiration society, or "bromance" as the press refers to it.

Finally, on July 27, 2016, Trump admitted, "I never met Putin." This is a classic Trumpism: two completely contradictory statements on the same subject, with no room for ambiguity. One of these declarations must be true, and the other false. And never even a hint of an apology or sense of embarrassment.

The similarities between Donald J. Trump and Vladimir Putin are striking. Although I will gladly defer to the psychological professionals for a full DSM-V diagnosis, it is abundantly clear to even the most casual observer that both men are egotistical narcissists who are doomed to view all world events -- either of great significance or trivial -- through the prism of their self-interest. They are both extremely thin skinned and overly sensitive to criticism. Trump, as he had repeatedly demonstrated, can be provoked by even the mildest of tweets from Elizabeth Warren, among others, which predictably sets him off on a Twitter rampage. He regularly lashes out at his foes, both real and imagined, like a spoiled four-year-old in a sandbox, not as a candidate for the leader of the free world. No wonder the press and the American public is beginning to wonder of he has the mental and psychological stability to be given access to the "black box" and the nuclear codes.

Putin is also another one to never forget a slight, and waits as long as it takes to seek his revenge. When President George W. Bush famously said when he first met Putin that he could see into the man's soul, Hillary Clinton publicly quipped that Bush could not have seen Putin's soul because he didn't have one. Why? Because he was a former KGB agent. This is but one small example of how, in Putin's eyes, Hillary Clinton disrespected him. Putin has also been deeply stung by Clinton's public and vocal opposition to Russia's territorial aggression in Ukraine, Georgia, and other countries, which resulted in severe damage to the Russian economy once the U.S. and its allies imposed sanctions.

Both Putin and Trump are also notorious bullies, "wannabe" tough guys who try to hide their essential cowardice by always telling the world how they are prepared to beat people up. Putin is subtle about it. He has cultivated a self-image of being a "man's man" by being periodically photographed riding horses bare-chested, or wrestling a series of handsome young men for exercise. (What is that all about!).

Trump just wants to hurt people and often brags about it. At his rallies, he repeatedly urged his adoring followers to "knock the crap out of" demonstrators. During the Democratic National Convention, he told a reporter that he wanted "to punch" some the Democratic speakers. He was unclear as to whether those aggressive urges were aimed at just the male speakers, or whether he was gender neutral and wanted to assault both men and women alike. How about that Katy Perry? What did he think of her unabashed admiration for Hillary Clinton? Did that drive him to rage? Perhaps he just wanted to rough her up a bit.

In typical bully fashion, Trump likes to threaten people from the safety of a studio armchair or from the podium at a rally when he is protected by the Secret Service, Corey Lewandowski (the one who roughed up a female reporter and then denied it), or a bevy of burly supporters.

Trump And The Pro-Russian Republican Platform

During the Republican National Convention, the RNC watered down the Republican Platform to make it more favorable to Russia. Specifically, according to the L.A. Times, a Trump surrogate intervened to eliminate a specific provision that would require the U.S. to provide arms to Ukraine in its fight with Russia. The platform also weakened language criticizing Russia for intervening in Ukraine.

Rachel Hoff, a member of the platform committee, was quoted by The Washington Post as saying: "It was troubling to me that they would want to water down language that supports a country that has been invaded by an aggressive neighbor." She added: "I think the U.S. should properly come to Ukraine's aid in that struggle. In the past, that would not be considered a controversial Republican position."

Suspicion as to the origin of this critical revision immediately fell on Paul Manafort, Trump's then Campaign Manager, who well knew that an explicit call for the U.S. to provide defensive military equipment to Ukraine could tip the scales in Ukraine's favor in its ongoing confrontation with Moscow in Crimea and eastern Ukraine.

As reported by Sally Bronston on "Meet the Press" on July 31, 2016, Manafort emphatically denied that anyone in the Trump campaign organization had any role in changing the language of the Republican Party platform relating to Ukraine. "It absolutely did not come from the Trump campaign," Manafort said. He also denied taking a personal role in altering the platform, saying "I had none. In fact, I didn't even hear of it until after our convention was over."

In an interview with ABC News, Trump himself claimed he was not personally involved in the platform change, saying, "I was not involved in that. I'd like to – I'd like to take a look at it. But I was not involved in that."

However, unlike what Manafort told *NBC News*, Trump did not completely rule out that his campaign or surrogates may have been involved. Asked if he knew what changes were made, Trump replied, "They softened it, I heard."

However, a few days later, *The Daily Beast* reported that Manafort's categorical denial as to having had any involvement in this policy change was false and that the Trump campaign went out of its way to dramatically alter the Republican Party's official and longstanding position on Ukraine.[19]

Manafort's account was contradicted by four sources in the room, both for and against the language. Eric Brakey, a Maine delegate who identifies as a non-interventionist, said he supported the change, which was pushed in part by the Trump campaign. "Some staff from the Trump campaign came in and… came back with some language that softened the platform," Brakey told *The Daily Beast*. "They didn't intervene in the platform in most cases. But in that case, they had some wisdom to say that maybe we don't want to be calling… for very, very clear aggressive acts of war against Russia."[20]

"They substantively changed it," Washington, D.C., delegate Rachel Hoff told *The Daily Beast*, who was present during the meeting. "It absolutely was my understanding that it was Trump staff." According to two Republican delegates, the Trump campaign's efforts were led in part by J.D. Gordon, a Trump campaign official and a former spokesman at the Pentagon. [21]

The Daily Beast further reported that records for the meeting seem to have disappeared. A co-chair for the national security platform subcommittee told *The Daily Beast* that the minutes for the meeting have been discarded. The Republican National Committee had no comment when asked whether this was standard procedure for all the subcommittees.

During the platform committee meeting where this Ukraine provision was being considered, pro-Cruz delegate Diana Denman proposed language that called for "providing lethal defensive weapons" to Ukraine. Her amendment was put on hold so that Republican staff could work with Denman on the language. What followed was a back and forth between Denman and the Trump campaign, according to Denman.

"They were over sitting in chairs at the side of the room," Denman said of two men who stated that they working for the Trump campaign, one of whom was Gordon. "When I read my amendment, they got up and walked over and talked to the co-chairmen and they read it. That's when I was told that it was going to be tabled."[22]

Denman says the two men took a copy of her amendment back to their chairs, then made calls on their cell phones. Later, she said the two members of Trump's team claimed to have called the campaign's New York headquarters, and that her amendment needed to be changed.

The Daily Beast further reported that when the language came back up, after consultation with Trump's staff, and in direct contradiction to Manafort's insistence to the contrary, the section called merely for "appropriate assistance" to Ukraine.

This change in wording was particularly controversial, given the fact that Manafort had previously worked for pro-Putin Ukrainian President Viktor Yanukovych, who was forced out of the country in 2014 and is now in Moscow plotting a return to power in Ukraine. Putin subsequently annexed Crimea and encouraged an ongoing conflict in eastern Ukraine.

The Daily Beast further reported that it was also an unusual move for a Trump aide to be hovering over the committee's deliberations on Ukraine. That's something that did not occur in other subcommittees, or on very many other issues. Boyd Matheson, a Utah delegate on the Constitution Subcommittee, said that the Trump campaign was "nowhere to be seen" during their deliberations. David Johnson, an Ohio delegate who worked on the Subcommittee on Jobs and the Economy, said that "nobody from the Trump campaign suggested that we do or not do anything."

The move, first reported by *The Washington Post*, alienated Republicans who have made up the party's foreign policy base for decades and indicated that the Trump campaign has a particular interest in Ukraine, where Manafort had previously worked for the pro-Russian President, Victor Yanukovich.

Trump's other senior foreign policy advisor, former Defense Intelligence Agency chief Michael Flynn, may have also influenced the decision to tone down the Republican platform so that it would be less objectionable to the Russians. Flynn was selected by Trump as one of his two advisors who would accompany him during his first classified intelligence briefing at the FBI's New York field office on August 17, 2016. The other advisor was New Jersey Governor Chris Christie.

Flynn raised eyebrows in the intelligence community when he decided to join Vladimir Putin at a luncheon in Moscow during December 2015. Flynn has been outspoken in favor of closer ties between the U.S. and Russia, notwithstanding its aggressive action in Ukraine and elsewhere. In interviews with *The Washington Post*, Flynn acknowledged that he had been paid to give a speech and attend a lavish anniversary party for the Kremlin-controlled RT television network in Moscow last year, where he was seated next to Russian President Vladimir Putin. [23] Asked why he would want to be so closely associated with a Kremlin propaganda platform, Flynn said he sees no distinction between RT and other news outlets. 'What's CNN? What's MSNBC? Come on!' said Flynn." In other words, Flynn was making the outlandish suggestion that CNN and MSNBC are propaganda outlets for the U.S. government, like the Voice of America, and were not independent news networks.

Flynn's outspoken criticism of U.S. policy towards Russia has dismayed most of his former colleagues, including retired Gen. Stanley A. McChrystal and retired Admiral Michael Mullen, a former chairman of the Joint Chiefs of Staff. According to *The Washington Post*, they have contacted Flynn and asked him to show greater restraint in his public comments. [24]

Carter Page is another senior Trump adviser on foreign policy matters who is an enthusiastic booster of Russian President Vladimir Putin's policies. As reported by *The Washington Post* on August 5, 2016, Page's praise for Putin and Trump at a June 2016 gathering of Washington foreign policy experts meeting with the visiting prime minister of India stunned the assembled group. Page apparently lauded Putin as stronger and more reliable than President Obama and lectured on the benefits that a Trump presidency would have on U.S.-Russian relations. [25]

The following month, Page gave a similar speech in Moscow during an address at the New Economic School commencement. Page criticized the U.S. and other Western countries for "imped[ing] potential progress through their often hypocritical focus on ideas such as democratization, inequality, corruption and regime change."

Page, who was little known before affiliating with the Trump campaign, worked for Merrill Lynch in Moscow from 2004 to 2007 and claimed to have an investment stake in Gazprom, the Russian-owned energy giant. He was an adviser "on critical transactions for Gazprom." In a two-hour interview with *Bloomberg News* in late March 2016, Page said he advised Gazprom on its largest deals.[26] His counsel included buying a stake in an oil and natural gas field near Russia's Sakhalin Island and the merging of two classes of Gazprom stock, one of which was restricted to foreigners and the other to Russians.

Page's financial interests were apparently severely damaged by the U.S. imposed economic sanctions placed on Russia after its annexation of Crimea and incursions into eastern Ukraine, as well as for its persistently poor record in the human rights area. According to *Bloomberg News*, Page's investment firm, Global Energy Capital, which had offices in New York close to Trump Tower, failed in its attempt to raise sufficient funds to invest in oil and gas deals in Russian and neighboring Turkmenistan.

Page was bitterly incensed by U.S. sanctions, which he held responsible for the inability of his company to move ahead with its business plans in that part of the world. He told *Bloomberg News*: "So many people who I know and have worked with have been so adversely affected by the sanctions policy." He also acknowledged that his own personal investments had suffered. "There's a lot of excitement in terms of the possibilities for creating a better situation [under a President Trump]," he added.

The reaction by foreign policy experts to Page's blatantly anti-U.S. comments and Trump's sharp tilt towards Russia, was swift and sharply critical, as reported by *The Washington Post*. "It scares me," said David Kramer who was responsible for Russia and Ukraine at the State Department during the George W. Bush administration. He called Page's and recent comments by Trump on the possibility of lifting sanctions against Moscow "deeply unsettling."[27]

Asked by *The Washington Post* to comment on Page's public statements and campaign role, Trump spokeswoman Hope Hicks said Page was an "informal foreign policy adviser" who "does not speak for

Mr. Trump or the campaign." However, Trump identified Page as one of his foreign policy advisers during a meeting at *The Washington Post* in March 2016.

Page has also made some bizarre posts on his blog for the Global Policy Journal, which alone raise serious questions about Trump's judgment in naming him as one of his foreign policy advisors. For example, on Feb. 10, 2015, he compared the February 2015 National Security Strategy rationale for imposing sanctions on Russia to an 1850 publication offering slaveholders guidance on how to produce "the ideal slave."

Page was also extremely critical of the Obama Administration's decision to add Igor Sechin, a Russian official, to its sanctions list in 2014. Page praised the Russian official, who, according to The Washington Post, is considered one of Putin's closest allies over the past 25 years. Page wrote: "Sechin has done more to advance U.S.-Russian relations than any individual in or out of government from either side of the Atlantic over the past decade."

In another blog post on March 31, 2015, titled "ISIS Response Self-help Principles for Would-be Warriors of the West", Page approvingly cites Dale Carnegie's classic "How to Win Friends and Influence People" as a strategy for dealing with the Islamic State.

Given the fact that Trump's senior advisors had a strong opinion favoring a more accommodating stance towards Putin and Russia, it is not surprising that the Trump campaign would want to water down the Republican platform. This would signal to the Russians that the U.S. would not provide military defense systems to Ukraine or other Eastern

European countries that were subject to Russian aggression and annexation of huge chunks of territory.

Trump's Approval Of Russian Aggression In Ukraine

Trump's admiration for Putin and all things Russian has inevitably led to a change in the way he has viewed Russian aggression in Ukraine and elsewhere.

Last September 2015, Trump's views on Russian aggression in Ukraine seemed to be in line with prevailing U.S. and Western European foreign policy, which firmly condemned Russia for failing to respect Ukraine's territorial integrity by annexing Crimea in March 2015, and by actively supporting the pro-Russian separatist movements in eastern Ukraine. When he spoke by video to a gathering of political and business elites in Kiev, Ukraine, he stated:

> "Our president is not strong and he is not doing what he should be doing for the Ukraine," Trump told the group of pro-Western businessmen, diplomats, and politicians. "I don't think you're getting the support you need."

During his comments in Kiev last September, Trump sharply rebuked the entire Western response to Russian aggression in Ukraine as wholly inadequate. "So far we have all lip service," Trump said.

Appearing on NBC's "Today" show on March 13, 2016 he said that the Russian land grab, which Obama and top European leaders denounced as a gross violation of international law, "should never have happened." Trump added: "We should definitely be strong. We should definitely do sanctions."

Speaking to a Conservative Political Action Conference, Trump darkly pronounced that Putin had seized "the heart and soul" of Ukraine. He predicted that if the U.S. and its allies did not take bold action, "that means the rest of Ukraine will fall."

However, by mid- 2016, after naming Paul Manafort as his Campaign Manager and Carter Page as his foreign policy advisor, Trump has reversed his position, now saying that he might recognize Crimea as Russian territory and lift punitive U.S. sanctions against Russia. Trump signaled that he was "going to take a look" at recognizing Russia's annexation of Crimea and lifting economic sanctions on Russia.

During an appearance on ABC's "This Week," Trump sounded like an apologist for Russia's iron grip on the territory, repeating the talking points that the Kremlin has been using in an attempt to justify its land grab of Ukrainian territory. "The people of Crimea, from what I've heard, would rather be with Russia than where they were," Trump said. To be sure, in March 2014, 95.5% of Crimean voters did cast ballots to join Russia. But the opposition groups and a significant portion of the Crimean residents, including most Crimean Tatars who are native to the area, boycotted the referendum, which the European Union declared "illegal and illegitimate."

The Trump campaign's dramatic policy shift regarding Ukraine is not terribly surprising given the fact that Manafort has been unabashedly pro-Russian for many years, especially since he worked on the pro-Russian campaign of former Ukraine President Victor Yanukovich in 2009-2010. In March 2016, Trump also announced that one of his foreign policy advisers would include Page, an investment banker who has criticized the Obama administration for "fomenting" Yanukovych's ouster, which infuriated Putin. Page, who has likened the U.S. role in Ukraine to Russian meddling in Canada, has extensive business ties in Russia and has vehemently decried the impact of Western sanctions against Moscow related to Ukraine. "So many people who I know and have worked with have been so adversely affected by the sanctions policy," Page told *Bloomberg Politics* in March 2016. "There's a lot of excitement regarding the possibilities for creating a better situation."

However, Manafort and Page apparently failed to adequately brief Trump about the basic geographical and geopolitical issues relating to Crimea. This caused massive confusion. For instance, Trump seemed to be ignorant of where Crimea exactly was located, and that it had been part of Ukraine.

On July 31, 2016, in an interview with ABC News, apparently not knowing that Crimea was part of Ukraine, Trump stated that Russian President Vladimir Putin was "not going to Ukraine…
you can mark it down." This caused widespread consternation, since Russia was already clearly "in Ukraine," having already annexed Crimea. Indeed, about one week earlier, Trump stated during a press conference that, as President, he would probably withdraw U.S. objections to the annexation of Crimea.

With those two brief statements, Trump revealed the depth of his ignorance of foreign affairs, at least that relating to Russia and Eastern Europe.

Russian Aggression in Crimea

Here are the facts. Until 2014, Crimea was part of Ukraine. During 2014, Russian military forces crossed the Russian-Ukrainian border into Crimea and effectively annexed it. Before invading, the Russian special forces were told to remove the identifying insignias on their uniforms, which led to the press references to them as "the little green men." Since then, the indigenous Crimean Tatar population has been subjected to a relentless campaign of persecution by the Russian occupying forces. All but one of their cultural and religious centers has been closed; use of the Tatar language has been severely restricted, and dozens of Crimean Tatars have been jailed, tortured, or simply made to "disappear."

Russian mistreatment of the Crimean Tatars actually dates back to 1944, when these indigenous peoples of the area were subjected to an intentional campaign of genocide and ethnic cleansing. Stalin and the Soviet leadership ordered the forcible deportation of the Crimean Tatars from Crimea, on the trumped up charge that the Tatars had collaborated with the Nazis. Many Crimean Tatar soldiers fighting with the Red Army were also detained.

Soviet motivations for the elimination of the Crimean Tatars included the strategic location of Crimea next to the Black Sea and close to Turkey. Another motivation was their close historical and cultural ties with Turkey. Since the Soviet Union had a long-term plan to annex the Ardahan and Kars provinces of Turkey, and to demand naval bases at the Turkish Straits, the deportation of the Crimean Tatars took place in preparation for a possible future Soviet-Turkish conflict.

At least 238,500 people were deported, mostly to the Uzbek Soviet Socialist Republic. This included the entire ethnic Crimean Tatar population. A large number of deportees (more than 100,000 according to a 1960s survey by Crimean Tatar activists) died from starvation or disease as a direct result of deportation. This was a clear-cut case of genocide and "ethnic cleansing."

The deportation began on May 18, 1944, in all Crimean-inhabited localities. The forced deportees were given only 30 minutes to gather personal belongings, after which they were loaded onto cattle trains and moved out of Crimea. The deportees were brought to central gathering stations in Simferopol and Bakhchysarai, and after a short waiting period, loaded on trains. At the same time, most of the Crimean Tatar men who were fighting in the ranks of the Red Army were demobilized and sent to forced labor camps in Siberia and in the Ural mountain region.

According to eyewitness accounts, the Russian NKVD officials forgot to deport the Crimean Tatars in the fishing villages of the Arabat Spit. On July 19, 1944, when Soviet authorities learned about these villages, orders were issued that no Crimean Tatar should be left alive within 24 hours. Following this, all inhabitants of these villages were locked up in an old and big boat, which sailed to the deepest part of the Azov Sea and was then sunk. Soviet soldiers waited in a nearby ship with machine guns.

The train journey of the deportees to the destinations was carried out under harsh conditions and resulted in a significant number of deaths. According to official Soviet data, 7,889 people, amounting to approximately 5% of the Crimean Tatar population was presumed dead during the deportation, but in all probability, these estimates were grossly understated. The removal was carried out in sealed box cars, and thousands of deportees died because of thirst. The cars were called "crematoria on wheels" by Crimean Tatars. The doors and windows were tightly bolted to prevent the entry of fresh air, there was no medical care and little food. This led to the deaths of mainly elderly people and children, who could not withstand the suffocating conditions and the lack of food. Grigorii Burlitskii, an NKVD officer overseeing the deportation who later defected, reported that "they were packed into wagons like sardines, the wagons were locked and sealed and put under the guard of military detachments." According to testimonies, the doors of the cars were only opened upon arrival to the Kazakh steppe, where the dead were dumped along the railway track, with the deportees not given the time to bury them.

The deportation was poorly planned and executed. Local authorities in the destination areas were not adequately informed about the scale of the matter and did not receive enough resources to accommodate the deportees. The lack of accommodation and food, the failure to provide proper clothing to help the deportees to adapt to new climatic conditions and the rapid spread of diseases further decimated the Crimean Tatar people during the first years of exile.

Upon their arrival in Central Asia, Crimean Tatars were forced to live in special settlement camps, surrounded by barbed wire. Leaving the camps was punished by five years of hard forced labor. Many Crimean Tatars were also made to work in the large-scale projects conducted by the GULAG system. In these forced labor camps, deportees were assigned the heaviest tasks available and awoken before dawn for 12-hour workdays.

In Uzbekistan, Stalin ordered the settlement of Crimean Tatars in kolkhozes (collective farms) sovkhozes(state-owned farms) and settlements around factories for industrial and agricultural production. The deportees partially provided the required workforce for the industrial development of the area. Regardless of their former profession and skills, Crimean Tatars were forced to do heavy labor. Their places of residence consisted of barracks, makeshift shelters, parts of factories and communal housing.

The Soviet government also efficiently destroyed all remaining traces of Tatar culture. This included the destruction of Tatar monuments and burning of Tatar manuscripts and books. Tatar mosques were converted into movie theaters and warehouses; gravestones of Tatars were used as building material. Exiled Crimean Tatars were banned from speaking of Crimea, and official Soviet texts, including the Great Soviet Encyclopedia, erased all references to them. When applying for internal passports, "Crimean Tatar" was not accepted as an existing ethnic group and those that designated themselves as "Crimean Tatars" were automatically denied passports.

Soviet authorities also ordered the renaming of all Tatar place names (including mountains and rivers), and a decree of the RSFSR Supreme Soviet Presidium on December 14, 1944, required the renaming of all districts and community centers to Russian-language names. In total, more than 1389 Crimean Tatar towns and villages were renamed.

The Soviet propaganda machine worked hard to hide the true nature of the deportation from the domestic and international media by falsely claiming that it was "voluntary." The deportations were referred to as "resettlement." Crimean Tatars were depicted as "bandits" and "thieves," and were accused of being Nazi agents.

On April 28, 1956, by the decree of the Supreme Soviet Presidium of the USSR, the Crimean Tatars were released from special settlement, accompanied by a restoration of their civil rights. In the same year, the Crimean Tatars started a petition to allow their repatriation to Crimea. They held mass protests in October 1966, but these were violently suppressed by the Soviet military. On June 21, 1967, after a meeting between representatives of the Soviet government and a Crimean Tatar delegation, prompt rehabilitation of Crimean Tatars was promised but never fulfilled. In August and September 1967, thousands of Crimean Tatars took to the streets to protest in Tashkent.

A decree of the Supreme Soviet Presidium was issued on September 5, 1967, exonerating the Crimean Tatars, but the Soviet government did nothing to facilitate their resettlement back to Crimea or to make reparations for the loss of lives and confiscated property. In 1968, a token 300 families were allowed to return, but this was only for propaganda purposes. Crimean Tatars, led by the Crimean Tatar National Movement Organization, were not allowed to return to Crimea from exile until the beginning of the Perestroika in the mid-1980s.

The Crimean Tatars began repatriating on a massive scale beginning in the late 1980s and continuing into the early 1990s. The population of Crimean Tatars in Crimea rapidly reached 250,000 and leveled off at about 270,000. There are believed to be between 30,000 and 100,000 remaining in exile in Central Asia.

Finally, in November 1989, after the end of the Cold War, the Soviet government acknowledged responsibility for this clear violation of international law. In November 1989, the Supreme Soviet of the USSR recognized the deportation as a crime against humanity of the highest degree. On April 21, 2014, following the annexation of Crimea by Russia, President Vladimir Putin of Russia signed a decree that "rehabilitated" Crimean Tatars and other ethnicities who suffered from Stalinist repressions in Crimea. However, this decree proved to be hollow, not only because there was no compensation, reparations or restitution offered, but also because Russia instituted a crackdown on Crimean Tatar dissidents who opposed the annexation and favored a continuing relationship with Ukraine. Leaders of the Crimean Tatar opposition have been subjected to prolonged arbitrary detention, which itself is a recognized violation of customary international law, and the general Crimean Tatar community has been subjected to a continuing reign of terror and Crimes Against Humanity. These crimes included arbitrary killings, arbitrary confiscation of property, state-sponsored and widespread theft of personal and real property, extortion and harassment of every possible variety.

Thus, the Crimean people –especially the Crimean Tatars -- have been subjected to longstanding abuses by Russia, with the 2014 annexation of Crimea being only the most recent episode. The annexation is also a flagrant violation of international law, which requires each nation state to respect the territorial integrity of its neighboring countries.

For these reasons, the U.S. and its allies have steadfastly denounced Russia's annexation of Crimea and have imposed heavy economic sanctions on Russia until it restores Crimea to its rightful place as part of Ukraine. Donald Trump either does not understand this or doesn't care.

Russian Aggression in Eastern Ukraine

At about the same time in 2014 that Russia was annexing Crimea, Russian forces also moved into eastern Ukraine in April 2014 to support the separatist pro-Russian insurgents in the Donbas region in their effort to create an "independent" republic aligned with Russia. More than 10,000 people have died in the ensuing conflict, and the atrocities and human rights violations that were perpetrated by the pro-Russian forces have been universally condemned by the U.S., its European allies, and by numerous human rights organizations.

During the armed conflict between Ukrainian government forces and insurgents in the Donbas region of Ukraine (the Donetsk and Lugansk Oblasts), numerous human rights and international law violations were commited by separatists affiliated with the so-called Donetsk People's Republic (DPR) and Lugansk People's Republic (LPR). In a report from the UN Human Rights Monitoring Mission, Ivan Šimonović, UN Assistant Secretary-General for Human Rights, wrote about targeted killings, torture, abduction, illegal detention, and intimidation of election officials in the self-proclaimed pro-Russian republics, and called for urgent action to prevent a Balkans-style war. He also warned of a humanitarian crisis due to a failure of social services in the region, and an exodus of people from affected areas. The UN also reported threats against, attacks on, and abductions of journalists and international observers, as well as the beatings and attacks on supporters of Ukrainian unity.

A similar report by Human Rights Watch said: "Anti-Kiev forces in eastern Ukraine are abducting, attacking, and harassing people they suspect of supporting the Ukrainian government or consider undesirable...anti-Kiev insurgents are using beatings and kidnappings to send the message that anyone who doesn't support them had better shut up or leave."[28]

The use of abductions as a method to maintain political power and to terrorize the local population into submission appears to have been one of the preferred abusive techniques utilized by the pro-Russian separatist leadership. In early July 2014, Amnesty International published a report based on evidence of beatings, torture, and abduction of activists, protesters and journalists by insurgents in the Donbas region. It said that "while most abductions appear to have a 'political' motivation,' there is clear evidence that kidnapping and torture are being used by armed groups to exert fear and control over local populations." The report also said that some people had been abducted for ransom. The report summarized its finding by stating that "the bulk of the abductions are being perpetrated by armed separatists, with the victims often subjected to stomach-turning beatings and torture."

A report by the United Nations OHCHR that was released on July 28, 2014, said that insurgent groups continued "to abduct, detain, torture and execute people kept as hostages in order to intimidate and to exercise their power over the population in raw and brutal ways." The report documents that at least 812 people have been abducted by the insurgents since mid-April, and said that "the majority are ordinary citizens, including teachers, journalists, members of the clergy and students."

A statement released on August 22, 2014, by the Lithuanian foreign minister said that the Lithuanian honorary consul in Luhansk, Mykola Zelenec, was abducted by pro-Russian insurgents and killed.

A report by Human Rights Watch said that the rebels had been "running amok...taking, beating and torturing hostages, as well as wantonly threatening and beating people who are pro-Kiev". It also said that the insurgents had destroyed medical equipment, threatened medical staff, and occupied hospitals. A member of Human Rights Watch witnessed the exhumation of a "mass grave" in Sloviansk that was uncovered after separatists retreated from the city.

Captured Ukrainian soldiers have been subjected to public humiliation and other abuses in violation of international law. Insurgents with bayonet-equipped automatic rifles in the City of Donetsk paraded captured Ukrainian soldiers through the streets on August 24, 2014, the Independence Day of Ukraine. During the parade, Russian nationalistic songs were played from loudspeakers, and members of the crowd jeered at the prisoners with epithets like "fascist." Street cleaning machines followed the protesters, "cleansing" the ground they were walking on. Human Rights Watch said that this was in clear violation of the common article 3 of the Geneva Conventions. The article forbids "outrages upon personal dignity, in particular, humiliating and degrading treatment". They further said that the parade "may be considered a war crime." On the following day, the insurgents tied a woman accused of being a spy to a lamppost. They wrapped her in a Ukrainian flag and had passers-by spit her, slap her, and throw tomatoes at her.

In October 2015, the DPR and LPR banned non-governmental organizations such as Doctors Without Borders and World Food Program from the territory that they control. A report released on March 3, 2016, by the Office of the United Nations High Commissioner for Human Rights (OHCHR) said that people that lived in separatist-controlled areas were experiencing "complete absence of the rule of law, reports of arbitrary detention, torture, and incommunicado detention, and no access to real redress mechanisms."

According to the United Nations Children's Fund (UNICEF), "The results of a psychosocial assessment of children in Donetsk Oblast in Eastern Ukraine are deeply troubling ... and indicate that about half of all children aged 7-18 have been directly exposed to adverse or threatening events during the current crisis." OSCE monitors spoke to refugees from Donetsk city in Zaporizhia. They said that men were "often not allowed" to leave the city, but were instead "forcibly enrolled in 'armed forces' of the so-called 'Donetsk People's Republic' or obliged to dig trenches."

By June 2015, the conflict had created 1.3 million internally displaced people (IDPs). According to the OHCHR, this number had grown to 1.6 million people by early March 2016.

As the shaky ceasefire implemented by the Minsk Protocol became increasingly untenable at the beginning of November 2014, it was reported that the number of people that had fled insurgent-held areas of Donbas had reached one and a half million. Those forced to stay in the region were primarily elderly, destitute, or otherwise unable to flee. Schools had been abandoned, and many had been converted into weapons depots or unlawfully used for other military purposes, as roughly half of the pre-war population of school-age children had left Donbas.

A map of human rights violations committed by the separatists called the "Map of Death," was published by the Security Service of Ukraine (SBU) in October 2014. The reported violations included detention camps and mass graves. Subsequently, on October 15, 2014, the SBU opened a case on "crimes against humanity" perpetrated by insurgent forces.

Amnesty International reported evidence of summary killings of Ukrainian soldiers on April 9, 2015. Having reviewed video footage, it determined that at least four Ukrainian soldiers had been shot dead "execution style." The AI deputy director for Europe and Central Asia said that "the new evidence of these summary killings confirms what we have suspected for a long time." AI also said that a recording released by Kyiv Post of a man, allegedly separatist leader Arseny Pavlov, claiming to have killed fifteen Ukrainian prisoners of war was a "chilling confession", and that it highlighted "the urgent need for an independent investigation into this and all other allegations of abuses."

Since the insurgents are basically nothing more than proxies for Russia, Putin, and other Russian leaders bear substantial responsibility for the War Crimes and human rights abuses committed by the insurgent forces in Eastern Ukraine. Donald Trump should at least know these facts before formulating a policy of appeasement regarding Russia's decision to carve off huge chunks of Ukraine. Moreover, by telegraphing his intention to lift economic sanctions against Russia, he is encouraging Putin to violate international law once again by moving into one or all three of the Baltic nations, or Poland, all of whom are U.S. allies and members of NATO. Trump justifies his acquiescence to Russian aggression by saying that he wants to avoid World War III, but this is the same kind of appeasement policy that encouraged Hitler to invade Poland and trigger World War II.

Apparently Donald Trump, who ironically tries to project the image of a strong and tough candidate, refuses to understand the lessons of history, which is that appeasement in the face of aggression, is more likely in the long run to lead to conflict, not peace.

Trump's Encouragement of Russian Espionage In the U.S.

On Friday, July 22, 2016, more than 20,000 stolen emails from the Democratic National Committee's computer servers were released, first by a supposed hacker (whose "identity" had actually been created by a Russian intelligence agency), and later by WikiLeaks. The emails, which showed that the DNC strongly favored Hillary Clinton over her rival Bernie Sanders, was incredibly embarrassing to the DNC on the eve of the Democratic Convention, further enraged the Sanders camp, and resulted in the sacking of the DNC Chair, Debbie Wasserman Schultz.

Computer experts, including the cybersecurity firm Crowd Strike, were able to identify the source of this cyber attack as two Russian intelligence agencies: the G.R.U., the Russian military intelligence service, and the more sophisticated Federal Security Service (FSS). The digital fingerprints of Russian intelligence were all over the hacked emails. For example, some of the documents had been passed through Russian computers before they were released ("dumped"); some had Russian language settings, and others bore Moscow time stamps.

The state-sponsored hacking of a major U.S. organization such as the DNC is a significant and dangerous breach of U.S. security. It marks a sharp escalation in Russia's willingness to engage the U.S. in cyber war, risking all types of unintended consequences and inviting retaliation on, for example, the computers controlling Moscow's power grid.

Up until now, the Obama Administration refrained from any direct retaliation against Russia for its attacks on the State Department and White House unclassified email systems, and its attacks on networks used by the Joint Chiefs of Staff. Obama never even publicly identified Russian intelligence as the source of those intrusions, even though the evidence that Russia was behind those attacks was fairly compelling. Such restraint in the face of repeated cyber attacks by Russia is admirable, especially given the general consensus among experts that cyber warfare can quickly escalate into more conventional forms of combat.

Everyone knows that the U.S. has the capability to turn off every light in Moscow without warning, but what is uncertain is how Russia would respond to such an escalation in the ongoing chess game of cyber intelligence gathering, which is practiced by both sides. The only reason why the U.S. has not strongly retaliated against Russian cyber hacking of U.S. government systems is that both countries still have a formidable nuclear arsenal. The doctrine of "mutually assured destruction" (MAD) that has kept the U.S. and Russian forces from engaging in a mutual nuclear missile exchange for the past several decades continues to keep Russia and the U.S. reasonably safe from a nuclear Armageddon.

In contrast, the United States has not been so restrained when it comes to cyber intrusions by other countries. The U.S. brought indictments against Chinese and Iranian hackers for thefts of intellectual property and attacks on American banks and imposed economic sanctions against North Korea in early 2015 for the attack on Sony Pictures Entertainment's computers.

The U.S. also has not been so restrained with regard to North Korea, which had the audacity to launch a cyberattack on Sony Pictures Entertainment just prior to the release of the film "The Interview." The film was a devastatingly funny comedy that portrayed Kim Jong Un, the Supreme Leader of North Korea in a very unflattering light (to put it mildly). Not only did the U.S. impose economic sanctions, but shortly after the Sony Pictures hack became public, the lights in North Korea's capital city mysteriously went dark for a short time period. The U.S. publicly wrote it off as "a coincidence," but U.S. government officials knowledgeable about this episode privately confirmed that the sudden power failure was just a warning shot across the bow of North Korea. The power failure was intended to let the lunatics running North Korea know that we could turn off the power grid there anytime we wanted. Of course, North Korea does not yet have offensive missiles that can reach the West Coast, so the risk of massive retaliation by North Korea was minimal. With Russia, the calculations are far more complex. Russia may be economically struggling, but it still has the Bomb. Lots of them.

Donald Trump has publicly displayed to understanding whatsoever regarding the threat posed by Russian cyber espionage, and the sophisticated analysis required in evaluating such a threat and possible responses.

Trump's immediate reaction to the suggestion that the leak was perpetrated by the Russian intelligence services was to dismiss it. Given his close relationship with Russia and its autocratic leader, Vladimir V. Putin, Trump's instinctive reaction was to defend Russia as his "friend" and ally, and to denounce the DNC for suggesting that Russia was to blame. Trump tweeted: "The new joke in town is that Russia led the disastrous DNC e-mails …because Putin like me." Later that same day, however, on Monday, July 25, 2016, when the evidence of a Russian hack emerged as clearly undeniable, Trump, speaking in Roanoke, Va., referred to the hack as having possibly been carried out by "Russia, one of our many, many friends…."

No truer words have ever been spoken. Russia and Putin are indeed among Trump's closest friends, and they are doing everything in their power, including conducting cyber warfare against the DNC and other American institutions, in a sophisticated and coordinated effort to get their friend elected as the next President of the United States. What a coup! Vladimir Putin pulling the strings in both Moscow and Washington! An impossible dream come true.

Hillary Clinton was quick to grasp the significance of the Russian hack and dump job. If Trump were elected President, it would be like "Christmas in the Kremlin." Russia, a third rate economic power posing as a world super-power, would have brought the greatest and most powerful country in history into its orbit as a satellite vassal state.

On Wednesday, July 27, 2016, Trump dispelled any doubt that his sympathies lay with Russia and its authoritarian President Putin by openly inviting the Russian intelligence services to publish Hillary Clinton's emails that they had already successfully stolen, and encouraged them to continue to engage in their cyber espionage against the former Secretary of State. Referring to the 30,000 emails that are missing from Secretary Clinton's private email server, Trump stated at a news conference: "Russia, if you're listening, I hope you're able to find the 30,000 emails that are missing. I think you will probably be rewarded mightily by our press."

Predictably, Mr. Trump's bizarre remarks unleashed a storm of criticism from both Democrats and Republicans. Not only was he urging a hostile power to violate American law by breaking into a private computer network, but he was also directly contradicting the Republican platform, saying that cyber espionage "will not be tolerated," and promising to "respond in kind and in greater magnitude" to all Chinese and Russian cyber attacks. A spokesman for Speaker Paul D. Ryan took issue with Mr. Trump's request for Russian assistance in his campaign against Hillary Clinton, characterizing Russia as "a global menace led by a devious thug." The spokesman, Brendan Buck, added: "Putin should stay out of this election."

CNN legal analyst Steve Vladeck said that, while Mr. Trump's comments were not tantamount to "treason," Trump may have transgressed a different federal law that makes it a crime for an individual to induce others to commit felonies involving physical force against American property, "which almost certainly includes cyberhacking."

Mr. Trump tried to modify his remarks encouraging the hacking of Mrs. Clinton's emails, unconvincingly arguing that he was only trying to get the Russians to turn over their hacked documents to the F.B.I. However, the unmistakable "take away" from the entire incident could only be that Mr. Trump seemed willing to go to any lengths – including the encouragement of espionage by a hostile foreign power – in order to get additional fodder for his campaign to undercut his Democratic opponent for the Presidency.

9

TRUMP AND HIS TEAM

Donald Trump's vetting process for his senior campaign staff appears to be something between extremely lax and non-existent. Paul Manafort came and went as his campaign chief and then campaign manager, after the full extent became publicly known regarding Manafort's connections with the former pro-Russian Ukrainian President and pro-Russian oligarchs, who apparently paid him over $12 million off-the-books to help steer Ukraine firmly into the Russian orbit.

Carter Page is another Trump advisor who is an unabashed fan of Putin and all things Russian. Page has worked in Moscow and has a financial interest in Gazprom, the Russian state-owned energy company. As reported in *The Washington Post* on August 5, 2016l, Page shocked a high-powered meeting of Washington foreign policy experts meeting with the visiting prime minister of India. According to the *Post,* Page apparently hailed Putin as stronger and more reliable than President Obama, and then spoke about the positive effect a Trump presidency would have on U.S.-Russia relations. The *Post* also reported that about one month later, Page gave a speech in Moscow that was sharply critical of U.S. policy. He has been sharply critical of the economic and financial sanctions that the U.S. and Western European countries have imposed on Russia for the Russian aggression resulting in the annexation of Crimea, which was part of Ukraine but is now a *de facto* part of Russia, albeit in violation of international law.

When it comes to Trump advisors with a direct pipeline to the Kremlin, Trump Senior Advisor Boris Epshteyn is the real deal. He is Russian-born and emigrated to this country from Moscow in 1993, which in and of itself does not make him a Putin surrogate planted in the Trump campaign. However, what is extremely troubling about Epshteyn is that, as an attorney and investment advisor, he has spent much of his professional career promoting investments in Russia in general, and the City of Moscow in particular. In an October 2013 conference in New York City called "Invest in Moscow!", Epshteyn put together panels that were mainly comprised of Moscow city government officials, like Sergey Cheremin, who heads up Moscow's foreign economic and international relations department.

Unlike the way that business is conducted in the U.S., investments in Russian companies, and investments in Moscow itself, do not take place without the green light and involvement of the Russian leadership, right up to the top, which is where President Putin stands. Kathryn Stoner, an expert in U.S.-Russian relations at Stanford University, was quoted by the New York Times on August 12, 2016, as explaining: "In Russia, where business and the state are so closely linked, business dealings automatically imply ties to people high up in government as well." In other words, Epshteyn would not have been given such access to Russian officialdom without having high-level contacts himself in the Kremlin.

If there was any doubt remaining that Epshteyn was a Russian agent in the Trump camp, such doubts were dispelled after he started speaking as Trump's surrogate on all matters relating to Russia and

Ukraine. Epshtyn adopted wholesale the disinformation disseminated by the official and unofficial news outlets about Russia's 2014 annexation of Crimea, which was – and under international law, still is – part of Ukraine. This illegal and forceful taking on the entire Crimean Peninsula has not been recognized by the U.S. or any of its allies. Nevertheless, appearing on CNN on July 31, 2016, Epshtyn took the position that "Russia did not seize Crimea." He added: "We could talk about the conflict that happened between Ukraine and the Crimea, it's an ongoing battle, but there was no seizure by Russia. That is an incorrect statement, characterization, of what happened."[1]

So what occurred in Crimea then, Boris? Did the poor suffering people of Crimea invite Russian unmarked troops to cross the border and occupy this entire section of Ukraine? That is the Russian propaganda line, which apparently is now the Trump line as well. When Hitler annexed the Sudetenland area of Czechoslovakia in March 1938, he ripped a page from a well-worn playbook used by despots and dictators throughout history, which is that the invasion and annexation of a neighboring territory were justified because the ethnic German-speaking natives there were being persecuted. Russia made the same argument about Crimea (substitute "Russian-speaking" for "German speaking"), and Putin's man in the Trump campaign (*i.e.*, Epshtyn) just parroted the party line.

With a phalanx of Russian and Russian-leaning foreign policy advisors such as Carter Page and Boris Epshtyn surrounding him, it has become increasingly clear that Trump, if elected President, will radically shift American foreign policy away from NATO and our Western

European allies towards Russia. This shift will inevitably lead not only to the abandonment of the U.S.'s opposition and economic blockage of Russia over the Crimean annexation, but also the inexorable gravitational shift of the rest of Ukraine and other Eastern European and Baltic nations back into the Russian orbit.

Another somewhat bizarre top Trump advisor is **Roger Stone**, a former consulting partner of Paul Manafort. Stone is a legendary "dirty tricks" political operative and a specialist in opposition research. He officially left the Trump campaign in August 2015, only two months after the campaign began. However, it has been reliably reported that Stone never actually left the campaign and that he is in frequent contact with Trump, and is one of his most influential (although informal) advisors. One of the reasons Stone had to cut his official ties with the Trump campaign is that his over-the-top conspiracy theories over the years are so outlandish that they tend to suck all of the air out of a campaign and cause it to lose all credibility.

As reported by *Media Matters* on May 9, 2016, Stone "is a discredited researcher and conspiracy theorist who claims the Clintons and Bushes secretly murdered dozens; the collapse of World Trade Center Building 7 is "suspicious"; President Lyndon Johnson killed President John F. Kennedy; President George H.W. Bush tried to assassinate President Ronald Reagan; and the Clintons killed John F. Kennedy Jr." Stone was always a big Richard Nixon fan and felt that he had been unfairly railroaded into resigning the Presidency after the Watergate Scandal broke. In 2007, Stone had Richard Nixon's face tattooed on his back. [2]

Stone has attracted controversy and chaos to almost every political campaign with which he has been affiliated over his long and less-than-illustrious career. In 1996, Stone resigned from a post as a volunteer spokesman in Senator Bob Dole's campaign for president after *The National Enquirer* wrote that Stone had placed ads and pictures in racy swingers publications. He also posted on a website seeking sexual partners for himself and his second wife, Nydia Bertrane Stone, whom he married in Las Vegas in 1992. Stone initially denied the report, but in a 2008 interview with *The New Yorker,* Stone finally admitted that the ads were authentic.

Just before the Republican National Convention, Stone formed a pro-Trump activist group, named "Stop the Steal", and threatened "Days of Rage" if Republican party leaders tried to deny the nomination to Trump. The *Washington Post* reported that Stone "is organizing [Trump] supporters as a force of intimidation," noting that Stone "has ... threatened to publicly disclose the hotel room numbers of delegates who work against Trump." Republican National Committee Chairman Reince Priebus was reported as saying that Stone's threat to publicize the hotel room numbers of delegates was "just totally over the line." During a live feed from the RNC, Stone was involved in a tense confrontation with Cenk Uygur, the co-founder of a group known as "The Young Turks."[3]

After Donald Trump had been criticized during the Democratic National Convention for his comments on Muslims by Khizr Khan, a Pakistani-American whose son received a posthumous Bronze Star and Purple Heart while serving in Iraq, Stone leaped to Trump's defense, accusing Khan of sympathizing with the enemy.

True to form, once the Trump presidential campaign got underway, Stone tapped into some of the conspiracy theories swirling around the darkest corners of the internet. Among those conspiracy were the theory that the electoral system is "rigged" and that if Trump lost, it would not be because he was beaten fair and square, but because the election was stolen from him. This should become known as the "Sore Loser Strategy." Heads I win and Tails you lose. Since Trump has a pathological fear of ever being labeled a "Loser," Stone's conspiracy theory is made to order. Stone has darkly predicted that if the election is stolen from Trump, there would be mass disobedience in the streets of America. In any other election year, Stone's paranoid fantasies would be written off as just more far right conspiracies to be filed away in the UFO file in Roswell, New Mexico. But for those of you who have just recovered from a year-long bout with amnesia, yes, this is 2016 and the Republican candidate for the presidency is Donald Trump. Strange but true.

Roger Stone has also evolved into Trump's political hit man. He can say whatever wild and crazy things that Trump may be thinking but has been counseled not to say himself. For example, as reported by *The Hill* on August 27, 2016, Stone told the *Financial Times* in an interview: "If Hillary wins, we're done as a nation. We'll be overrun by hordes of young Muslims, like Germany and France, raping, killing, violating, desecrating."[4]

Trump's new campaign chief executive, Stephen K. Bannon – Manafort's replacement -- got off to a rocky start in late August 2016 when it was disclosed that he had just changed his voter registration address in Florida as reporters were preparing a story about how he was registered at an address where he did not live.

As reported by *The Washington Post*, on Thursday, August 25th, Bannon's registration information was changed from an address in Miami-Dade County to Sarasota County, according to Carolina Lopez, the deputy supervisor of elections in Miami-Dade. On Friday morning, August 26, 2016, the *Guardian* reported that Bannon had been registered to vote at an address in Miami-Dade where he did not reside, which, if he had actually voted there, would have been a violation of the state election laws. The Miami-Dade property owner, Luis Guevara, told the Guardian that "nobody lives there." The report said Bannon formerly rented the house for use by Diane Clohessy, one of his ex-wives.

A Trump campaign spokesperson provided a statement from someone who said Bannon had lived there but did not respond to a question about why he changed his registration to the new address.

The Trump campaign also denied that Bannon made any anti-Semitic remarks after it was reported that he had said that he didn't want his twins to attend a school that had too many Jews. The *New York Daily News* reported Friday, August 26, 2016, that Bannon's ex-wife said in a 2007 court statement that Bannon didn't want their twin daughters attending a school because too many Jews attended. "The biggest problem he had with Archer [School for Girls in Los Angeles] is the number of Jews that attend," she said in her statement, which was reported in the *New York Daily News*. "He stated that he doesn't like the way they raise their kids to be 'whiny brats' and that he didn't want the girls going to school with Jews," Bannon's ex-wife wrote, according to the *Daily News*.

It was further reported that Bannon had been charged with misdemeanor domestic violence 20 years ago against his ex-wife. In the domestic violence case, as reported by *The Washington Post,* Bannon was accused of trying to prevent or dissuade the victim or a witness of a crime (i.e., his then wife) from reporting it. The crime was inflicting injury on a cohabitant or other closely associated person; and battery, according to court records in Southern California, where his ex-wife lived at the time. The case was eventually dismissed.

In an interview on August 26, 2016, with ABC News, Kellyanne Conway, Trump's campaign manager, said that she did not know whether Trump was aware of the prior domestic violence case against Bannon. "I don't know what he was aware of with respect to a 20-year-old claim where the charges were dropped," Conway said. "So that's all I know about is what I read.".

This incident highlights a serious flaw in Trump's management and hiring policies for senior staff. The customary and longstanding policy of most campaigns and companies are to do background checks that "vet" their senior staff *before* they are hired, not to wait for the media to do the background checking *after* the person is hired. If Trump were to actually be elected as President, he would have thousands of appointments literally to make, not only his Cabinet members but managers at all levels of every executive department. If Trump took the same lax approach to such appointments, it can be reasonably certain that chaos would ensue. But maybe that is part of his master plan.

10

TRUMP AND THE "SECOND AMENDMENT PEOPLE"

On Tuesday, August 9, 2016, at a rally in North Carolina, Donald Trump sent out yet another shock wave by implying that Second Amendment advocates should use their weapons if they didn't like Hillary Clinton's Supreme Court selections. He prefaced these remarks by falsely charging that "Hillary wants to abolish, permanently abolish the Second Amendment."

Trump then added: "If she gets to pick her judges, nothing you can do, folks." Almost as an afterthought, he added: "Although [for] the Second Amendment people, maybe there is, I don't know."

In other words, Trump was suggesting that the assassination of Hillary Clinton was an option to be considered in order to stop her from carrying out her gun safety agenda.

While shocking, Trump's remarks were not particularly surprising given his longstanding advocacy for the use of violence as a problem-solving tool. As Anna North wrote in an opinion piece in the *New York Times* on August 11, 2016, Trump has made numerous statements at recent rallies urging his supporters to engage in physical violence against protesters. Last November 2015, for example, Trump said: "Maybe he should have been roughed up," referring to a protester: "Because it was absolutely disgusting what he was doing."

In February 2016, he told a crowd: "If you see somebody getting ready to throw a tomato, knock the crap out of them, would you?

Seriously." He also promised to pay the legal fees for anyone who followed his advice. Later that same month, he just could not resist articulating his instinctual response to a protester: "I'd like to punch him in the face."

In March 2016, he reminisced about the "good old days" when men were men and they knew how to deal with protests. Without being very specific, Trump told the crowd at a rally that "they used to treat them very, very rough. And when they protested once, you know, they would not do it again so easily." So much for the First Amendment's freedom of speech. In Mr. Trump's universe, First Amendment protections apparently do not extend to peaceful protesters at rallies.

Many of Trump's supporters use more direct language as if to confirm to their candidate that they get his message loud and clear. "Kill her," they shout at rallies as if on cue when Hillary Clinton's name is mentioned. At the Republican National Convention, the chants were slightly toned down, advocating that perhaps her life should be spared; convention-goers shouted: "Lock her up!" Al Baldasaro, a New Hampshire Trump delegate, however, cried out for capital punishment for Secretary Clinton's offenses, suggesting that she be "put in the firing line and shot for treason." The Secret Service took note and immediately started an investigation.

Apparently many Trump people cannot distinguish between mere rhetoric and a call to take direct action.

Facing a withering storm of protest, Mr. Trump backtracked over the next few days, lamely explaining that he was only talking about the mysterious "power of unification." He claimed he was only suggesting that gun-rights advocates use their power at the ballot box to stop Hillary Clinton and her supposed opposition to the Second Amendment rights of homegrown terrorists and the mentally unstable to buy and use AK-47 assault rifles without background checks or other restrictions.

For many years, right-wing gun rights conspiracy theorists have opaquely suggested that gun owners should always maintain their "Second Amendment options," which is the dog whistle code for fringe groups to consider rising up in armed rebellion if things do not go well for them on election day. Now Trump has brought these dangerous fringe fantasies into the political mainstream. So when Trump talks about "Second Amendment people" everyone knows exactly what he is suggesting. He is suggesting that his supporters go one giant step beyond mere physical violence against protesters to the use of guns and live ammo to accomplish their twisted vision of what Amerika should be.

Republican rhetoric has radically changed over the years. Just eight years ago, Senator John McCain of Arizona told a man at an Arizona town hall meeting who said he was "scared" about an Obama presidency that Obama "is a decent person and a person that you do not have to be scared as president of the United States." At the same session, when a woman told Senator McCain that she couldn't trust Mr. Obama because "he's an Arab," McCain corrected her. "No ma'am," he replied. "He's a decent family man, a citizen that I just happen to have disagreements with on fundamental issues. And that's what this campaign is all about."

It is extremely unlikely that we will ever hear that same degree of statesmanship from Mr. Trump.

Patti Davis, the daughter of Ronald and Nancy Reagan, eloquently summed up what many were thinking after Trump made his incendiary "Second Amendment people" comment:"

> To Donald Trump: I am the daughter of a man who was shot by someone who got his inspiration from a movie, someone who believed if he killed the President the actress from that movie would notice him. Your glib and horrifying comment about "Second Amendment people" was heard around the world. It was heard by sane and decent people who shudder at your fondness for verbal violence. It was heard by your supporters, many of whom gleefully and angrily yell, "Lock her up!" at your rallies. It was heard by the person sitting alone in a room, locked in his own dark fantasies, who sees unbridled violence as a way to make his mark in the world, and is just looking for ideas. Yes, Mr. Trump, words matter. But then you know that, which makes this all even more horrifying.[1]

Thomas L. Friedman reminded us in his August 9, 2016 piece in the *New York Times* that the assassination of Israeli Prime Minister Yitzhak Rabin started with irresponsible accusations by his right-wing opponents, who called him a "traitor" and "a Nazi" for wanting to make peace with the Palestinians and, in the process, return part of Israel to them. They weren't actually telling people to assassinate Rabin, but to their rabid followers, it was the natural result. What else do you do to a latter-day Nazi?

As Friedman pointed out in his *Times* article, in the movie "Rabin: The Last Day," by Israeli director Amos Gitai, now-Prime Minister Benjamin Netanyahu, the opposition leader at the time, is shown in historical footage addressing a right-wing rally from Jerusalem's Zion

TRUMP AND THE SECOND AMENDMENT PEOPLE

Square, where protesters below shouted for the death of the "traitor" Rabin, holding photomontage posters of Rabin dressed in an SS uniform.

As Friedman noted, words can kill, since people with a penchant for violence cannot distinguish between "political stagecraft" and a signal to actually go out and kill the object of scorn. Friedman added: "People are playing with fire here, and there is no bigger flamethrower than Donald Trump."[2]

TRUMP AND GUNS

Donald Trump has consistently demonstrated that he will oppose any sensible restrictions on gun safety. In a speech at the National Rifle Association convention on May 20, 2016, Trump promised to do everything in his power to eliminate gun-free zones, including those applying to schools. He has promised to do away with gun-free zones on his "first day."

On May 22, 2016, two days after he spoke at the NRA convention, Trump expressed the view that "in some cases, teachers should have guns in classrooms, frankly."

Two days later, Trump stated that he wanted armed "school resource officers" to have guns in schools.

In response to the spate of terrorist attacks in Europe and the U.S., Trump expressed the view that more guns would save lives. He repeatedly has stated that he wished there were other armed individuals present during terror attacks so that they could fight back. "I think it would've been a lot better if they had guns in that room, somebody could protect," Trump said after the San Bernardino shooting in December 2015. "They could've protected themselves if they had guns." He repeated this view in June 2016 after the deadly shooting in Orlando, Florida at a gay nightclub. [1]

In the wake of the deadly shooting in Orlando, Florida at a gay nightclub in June, Trump reiterated this view. One day after the attack, during which an armed guard at the club was unable to stop the gunman, he stated in a TV interview:

> It's too bad that some of the young people that were killed over the weekend didn't have guns, you know, attached to their hips, frankly, and you know where bullets could have flown in the opposite direction. It would have been a much different deal. I mean, it sounded like there were no guns. They had a security guard. Other than that there were no guns in the room. Had people been able to fire back, it would have been a much different outcome.[2]

On June 15, 2016, Trump reiterated the opinion that the outcome in Orlando would have been different if some of those in the nightclub "had guns strapped to their waist or strapped to their ankle."

This position went too far for even the NRA, which objected to the idea of arming club goers. Just hours after the NRA questioned Trump's position, he dutifully fell into line and "walked back" his position that club patrons should be allowed to bring weapons into nightclubs. "I was obviously talking about additional guards or employees," Trump tweeted.

In short, Trump's position on guns is consistent with the longstanding position of the NRA, which is identical to that of the Republican Party: There should be virtually no restrictions on gun sales and ownership, even if the gun purchaser is on a terrorist "no fly" list.

12

TRUMP AND THE VETERANS

In January 2016, Trump boycotted a debate held on *Fox News* in advance of the Iowa caucuses. Instead, he held a fundraiser in Iowa for veterans, bragging that he had raised $6 million for the veterans and that he had contributed $1 million of his own money.

In May 2016, approximately four months after the fundraiser, the *Washington Post* starting asking the Trump campaign what had happened to the money. The *Post* discovered that Trump had not, in fact, raised $6 million as he had claimed, and that Trump had not even made the $1 million contribution that he claimed he had made. [1]

Trump responded by holding a press conference on Tuesday, May 31, 2016, announcing that he had given away all the money that he had raised four months earlier. At the same time, he attacked the news media for even raising the question as to what had happened to the money. As it turned out, however, Trump's press conference dug an even deeper hole regarding this veterans issue.

The *Associated Press* reported the same day that it had made phone calls to 41 of the veterans' groups that would have been likely recipients of Trump's largesse. About half of those that responded reported having received checks from Trump within the past week, typically dated May 24, 2016, the same day that *The Washington Post* had published the story questioning whether Trump had actually distributed all of the money.

In other words, Trump lied about contributing $1 million of his own money to veterans' charities and lied about having raised $6 million for them. Only after he was caught in these lies did Trump reluctantly part with the $1 million from his own pocket and cut checks to various charities for the amount (less than $6 million) that was actually raised. The entire sordid episode speaks volumes not only about the contempt that Trump harbors for the veterans and their charities but also about his almost compulsive penchant for prevaricating on virtually every subject.

13

TRUMP AND THE ELECTORAL SYSTEM

Donald Trump has repeatedly suggested that the electoral system is "rigged" against him and that "crooked Hillary" and the Democrats were planning to steal the election. In a campaign stop in Altoona, Pennsylvania, Trump told an overwhelmingly white audience that he had identified "certain sections of the state as likely targets for voter fraud." Although he did not specifically identify which sections he was referring to, it can be reasonably assumed that he was referring to Philadelphia and other large cities which have a high percentage of African-American voters.

Trump has good reason to worry about the election results if there is a large minority voter turnout this November. According to *NBC News*, as of August 23, 2016, Trump was trailing among black voters with only 8% support, as compared to 87% for Hillary Clinton. NBC also reported that Trump was behind among Hispanic voters, with 22 percent compared to 73 percent who support Clinton. Asian Americans also overwhelmingly support Clinton, with only 23 percent support compared with 66 percent favoring Clinton.

Trump has also warned during the campaign that recent court rulings striking down restrictive voter ID laws that would suppress the vote in minority and lower economic areas were part of a plot to steal the election from him. He speculated that, without tight restrictions requiring voter ID, certain people could vote up to fifteen times, and thus enable the Democrats to steal the election. "Go down to certain areas and watch and study and make sure other people don't come in and vote five times,"[1] Trump advised.

As the *New York Times* editorial board correctly noted on August 23, 2016, "the crime the [voter ID] laws were meant to prevent – voting by fraudulent voters with fake IDs – is a Republican myth, concocted for partisan reasons. There is no evidence that such fraud exists on any scale, only a handful of isolated instances." The real intent behind these restrictive laws is to suppress voting by blacks and Hispanics, who overwhelmingly have voted Democratic.

According to an *NBC News* report on August 22, 2016, the Trump campaign asked visitors to its website to sign up to be a "Trump Election Observer." Those who do sign up receive an email stating: "We are going to do everything we are legally allowed to do to stop crooked Hillary from rigging this election. Someone from the campaign will be contacting you soon."

According to *NBC News*, a Trump supporter in Florida took a more direct approach to this transparent attempt to intimidate and suppress minority voters from reaching the polls. He tweeted: "We gonna be watch'n fer shenanigans … & haul ya away," above a photograph of a pickup truck with a cage in the truck bed." In any other election year, such threats of vigilante action could be written off as just an inappropriate attempt at humor. But with Trump making voter suppression a central part of his campaign strategy, such dark threats harken back to the days when restrictive "poll taxes" and an occasional lynching were used in the Jim Crow southern states to intimidate

African-Americans and keep them far away from the polls on election day.

The U.S. Department of Justice is inadvertently cooperating with Trump's strategy by announcing that it is cutting back on the number of poll watchers it will be deploying around the country this November on election day. The DOJ says that such a decision was required by the Supreme Court's 2013 ruling in *Shelby County v. Holder*, which significantly weakened the Voting Rights Act. However, the DOJ has invited international observers from the Organization for Security and Cooperation in Europe (OSCE) to monitor the election, as it has during the past three presidential elections. OSCE has monitored elections in Russia, Ukraine and other countries.

However, the presence of OSCE monitors in certain parts of the country this election year may actually lead to disruptions of the electoral process since certain local officials have vowed in the past to arrest any such foreign observers, and will likely do so again this year. For example, Greg Abbot, who is now governor of Texas, threatened in 2012 when he was the Attorney General of the state that he would have OSCE observers arrested if they showed up in his state.

In addition to his voter suppression strategy, Trump is mounting an attack on the very integrity of the electoral system, which is the bedrock of our democracy. If the electoral system is "rigged," as Trump repeatedly claims, then the results (only if Clinton is elected President, but not if Trump is elected) will have been fraudulently obtained and should be considered to be illegitimate.

Roger Stone, a former partner of Paul Manafort and an adviser to the Trump campaign, has gone so far as to darkly suggest that if the election is stolen from Trump, there would be mass disobedience in the streets of America. In other words, Trump is preparing his "Second Amendment people" to take to the streets (or the hills) and challenge all civil authority if Trump is not elected.

Donald Trump is calling for volunteers to watch the polls in November, and he is making no bones about why. "Help me stop Crooked Hillary from rigging this election!" says the application form on his campaign website. There are so many lies and delusions flowing daily from the Trump campaign that it's easy to miss the times when the Republican nominee is not just ludicrous, but dangerous. This is one. Mr. Trump has seized on the charge that Hillary Clinton plans to win by cheating. He has said it before. but he keeps on saying it. This looks like a pre-emptive face-saving, effort, of course — getting an excuse ready if he loses badly. But it's worse than that. Mr. Trump has been attacking recent court decisions striking down utterly unjustified state voter identification laws that are attempts by Republican legislatures to hinder black and Latino voters, who tend to vote Democratic.

A more immediate concern is what happens on Nov. 8, 2016 when squads of Trump volunteers fan out to defend their candidate's presumed victory. It does not seem far-fetched to expect that signatures will be pointlessly challenged, and citizens intimidated and inconvenienced, that the ruckus of the Trump campaign will spread to polling places around the country.

The anger Mr. Trump is whipping up is not a small phenomenon. A Pew Research Center poll this month found that an amazing 30 percent of registered voters who support Mr. Trump have "little or no confidence" that their own vote will be counted accurately. Only 11 percent of Trump supporters believe that votes across the country will be accurately counted.

Senator John McCain made similar warnings in 2008, and charges of cheating go back at least to 2000 in Florida during a close national election. And long before Mr. Trump entered the presidential race, Republican legislators were busy passing voter ID laws based on the fallacy of widespread fraud.

Trump has merely taken this Republican myth of fraudulent minority voting to a new extreme. He is trying to whip his most die-hard supporters into a frenzy with images of the Clinton campaign dispatching thousands, if not millions, of African Americans and foreigners into booths across the country to fake their votes for Clinton, over and over again.[2]

Now, more than ever, the country needs responsible political leaders and the courts to defend and expand voting rights, rather than sitting silently while Mr. Trump further demolishes public confidence in the foundations of our electoral system.

14

TRUMP, HIS CHARITABLE CONTRIBUTIONS AND HIS TAXES

Donald Trump has steadfastly refused to release copies of his tax return. He is the only candidate from a major party for President to refuse to do so.

The release of a presidential candidate's tax returns has been a national tradition since 1972 when Richard M. Nixon held that office. Nixon was the president who famously declared on TV during a November 17, 1973, address to the American people that "I am not a crook," before resigning his office shortly after that in the midst of the Watergate scandal.

Ironically, Nixon's tax returns proved to be part of his undoing. In his taxes for 1969, Nixon claimed a deduction of more than $500,000 for 1000 boxes of documents that he had donated to the National Archives. However, as it turned out, and as detailed in an opinion piece by Mitchell Zuckoff in the *New York Times* on August 5, 2016.[1] Although the deed formally giving the papers to the National Archives was dated March 27, 1969, it was discovered that the deed had not actually been signed until April 1970, nine months after presidential document donations had lost nearly all of their tax benefits. In other words, the records supporting Nixon's huge tax deduction had been falsified. It turned out that he was a crook. Perhaps the past is prolog.

Why does Trump adamantly refuse to disclose his tax returns? It certainly has little or nothing to do with a current tax audit by the IRS. An audit does not prevent an individual from publicly disclosing his or her tax returns. That is just an excuse.

The reason why Trump does not want to disclose his tax returns is, quite simply, that there is information on those returns that he does not want the public to know about. He does not want to suffer the fate of Mitt Romney, who delayed the release of his tax returns during the 2012 presidential campaign, and then was criticized by the Democrats for having paid so little in taxes. This is clearly on Trump's mind. He told *Fox News* in July 2016 that after Romney finally released his tax returns after a long delay, "they [the Democrats] found a little sentence and they made such a big deal. He might have lost the election over that."[2]

Yes, Mr. Trump, words can matter, and little sentences can matter, especially when they are contained in tax returns.

Tax returns can tell you a lot about a person, and when that person is running for the office of President of the United States, where that person will be making important financial and economic decisions, the American people are entitled to know something about how the candidate has handled his or her own finances. Tax returns tell you how much the candidate has made in the past? How much in taxes did he (or she) pay? What tax rate was used to compute those taxes? Do the tax returns reflect any questionable business or financial affiliations with -- let's say, Russian companies, investors or oligarchs -- that may explain why the candidate is so favorably disposed to Russia and its current President? Do the tax returns reveal any other conflicts of interest that the

TRUMP, HIS CHARITABLR CONTRIBUTIONS AND HIS TAXES

American people should know about in evaluating the candidate's proposals to, for example, widen the tax loopholes for real estate developers?

Tax returns also tell you whether a person has given anything to charity, and if so, how much. This is an issue for Trump since he regularly trumpets the claim that he is a very generous person and gives millions to charity. However, as David Fahrenthold of *The Washington Post* reported on June 28, 2016, and subsequent articles, aside from the $1 million he gave to a non-profit group helping veterans' families in May 2016 under pressure from the media to make good on his promise to do so, Trump may only have given one personal charitable donation since 2009, fifteen years ago.

During the past 15 years, Trump has repeatedly promised to make donations from the earnings of "The Apprentice", Trump Vodka, Trump University, and two books he has written. An analysis by the *Post* estimates that if Trump had honored his pledges to donate these earnings from his various enterprises, Trump's charitable donations would have exceeded $8.5 million.

During that same 15-year time period, the *Post* reported that Trump had, in fact, donated about $2.8 million through a foundation that he had set up to give money away, but records showed that Trump himself had not given any funds to the foundation since 2008. The organization's money had come from other sources. [3]

According to the *Post,* Trump and his staff repeatedly insisted that Trump had made charitable contributions separate and apart from the Trump Foundation, but there was no way to confirm this since no details were provided and none of Trump's tax returns were released. Finally, the Trump campaign tried to make this issue go away by revoking the *Washington Post's* press credentials to cover his events.

Yes, barring news organizations access to information is one way of dealing with troublesome reporters asking difficult questions. But it is probably not good for the country or consistent with the principles underlying the First Amendment's freedom of the press. What kind of precedent does that set for the future? What if President Trump barred most major news organizations (except Fox News and Breitbart News of course) from White House press conferences? That certainly would have a chilling effect on the First Amendment's freedom of the press clause. However, press conferences would look a lot more organized, if not staged. Instead of multiple reporters shouting out questions at the same time and competing for the President's attention, we could have more Putinesque press conferences, where everything is carefully staged and the state media reporter's questions cleared in advance.

Fortunately, the *Post* did not give up in its quest for the truth regarding Trump's charitable giving (or lack thereof). Post reporters tenaciously dug back into records going back to the 1980s, and contacted 188 charities and nonprofits that had some connection with Trump in the past and would have been likely candidates for his self-declared largesse. These included recipients of Donald J. Trump Foundation monies, charities that Trump had commented on in the past, such as charities dedicated to fighting AIDS or multiple sclerosis, two causes that Trump had promised to contribute to from his book royalties. Well, it was an excellent idea. Isn't it the thought that counts? Not really. In reality, as

TRUMP, HIS CHARITABLR CONTRIBUTIONS AND HIS TAXES

we all know, saying you are going to do something good and positive and actually doing it are two very different things. There is many a slip between the cup and the lip.

What were the results of the *Post's* investigation? "In recent years, Trump's follow-through on his promises has been seemingly nonexistent." The *Post* added: "The search turned up just one donation in that period — a 2009 gift of between $5,000 and $9,999 to the Police Athletic League of New York City." Trump's charitable foundation had given at least $2.8 million, but as the Post pointed out, this was a drop in the bucket compared to what other billionaires give to charity. For example, the June 28, 2016 Post article noted that hedge fund billionaire Stanley Druckenmiller, who is ranked just behind Trump on the *Forbes* rankings of net worth, gave $120 million to his foundation in 2013 alone.

Bottom line? The *Post* summed it up the best: "What has set Trump apart from other wealthy philanthropists is not how much he gives — it is how often he promises that he is *going* to give." And then reneges on those promises.

Trump's misrepresentations about his charitable giving have less to do with money and more to do with his character and honesty. Since I am a New Yorker, and we pride ourselves on saying it like it is, let me be candid: Trump is a con man and BS artist, and always has been.

Good. I feel better now. Let us move on.

In the case of Donald Trump, there is another major reason why his tax returns should be disclosed. Mr. Trump repeatedly brags that one of his qualifications for being President is that he has been "hugely" successful in business and fabulously wealthy. Over the years, he has had a longstanding dispute with *Forbes* and other financial periodicals, who rank billionaires based on their net worth not the amount of press coverage they receive. *Forbes* has consistently taken the position that Trump is actually worth a lot less than he says he is. This has infuriated Trump, who has spent an inordinate amount of time and money trying to convince *Forbes* of the error of its way. *Forbes* has been unmoved.

Thus, in Mr. Trump's case, the issue of what he is worth has blossomed into an issue of credibility. If he is worth the $10 billion he says he has, more power to him. But if he is worth a lot less, and has been lying about it, isn't it much more likely than not that he will be willing to lie about other things also? This is called credibility (or lack thereof).

Hypothetically, even if Trump had some legitimate reason for not disclosing his tax returns for the years 2009 through 2015 (which he does not), this excuse would have nothing to do with his tax returns for prior years, which are *not* being audited. So what is he hiding?

Trump perhaps gave us a hint in a May 2016 interview with ABC's George Stephanopoulos. Trump remarked that his tax rate was "None of your business," adding: "I fight very hard to pay as little tax as possible."[4] This remark fueled speculation that Trump actually paid little or no personal income tax." *Fortune* commented on August 5, 2016 that "if Trump pays little or no tax, the tens of millions who pay income taxes are effectively paying his way."

It would not be surprising if it turned out that Trump was not paying any taxes. Some of his tax returns from the 1970s are, in fact, available, and in 1978 and 1978, he paid no taxes since he actually reported losses those years. In 1984, according to a *Washington Post* article on August 1, 2016, Trump said no personal income on his federal tax return for that year, although he reported capital gains from the sale of a condominium unit. [5]

During at least two years in the early 1990s, as reported by *Politico,* Trump appears to have paid no personal income taxes, or at least next to nothing. *Politico's* conclusions were drawn from documents on Trump's tax liabilities in 1991 and 1993 filed with the New Jersey Division of Gaming Enforcement and the Casino Control Commission. When *Politico* asked Trump questions about his not paying any income taxes in the early 1990s, a Trump spokesperson commented: "Welcome to the real estate business."[6]

This may be the key to one of Trump's major concerns about releasing his tax returns. The current tax codes are extremely favorable to real estate developers. As the New York Times explained in a September 1, 2016 article, "Thanks to some major loopholes in the existing tax code that treat real estate developers as a special privileged class, it's entirely possible (even likely) that Mr. Trump pays little or no federal income tax." [7]

It is extremely relevant for the public to know whether Trump is taking advantage of these generous loopholes available to real estate developers, because his new tax proposal would even add to those tax breaks, depriving the U.S. Treasury of an estimated $1 trillion in tax revenue over a ten- year period. Other proposed tax cuts by Trump and the Republican platform would generally benefit high-income earners, such as Trump, and if he is elected president and his tax plan in implemented, he would presumably benefit from those provisions as well. According to the *Times*, "even conservative Republican tax experts have denounced the particular real estate measures Mr. Trump has outlined." According to economist Douglas Holtz-Eakin, as quoted by the *Times,* "If you want to create a recipe for an abusive tax shelter, take those elements and bake for 15 minutes." [8]

One such loophole already on the books is the "carried interest" deduction, which allows real estate partners and hedge fund managers to convert ordinary income into capital gains, which are taxed at a lower rate. Trump has proposed abolishing this loophole, which might make him look like a tax populist at first blush. However, with a deft sleight-of-hand, Trump, in his "Tax Reform That Will Make America Great Again," proposes even more favorable tax breaks that make the carried interest deduction irrelevant.

For example, Trump's proposed new tax rate of 15 percent on all corporate and business income, is even lower than the current capital gains rate of 20 percent on profits from the sale of assets. In contrast, the tax rate on ordinary income is around 40 percent.

In addition, although Mr. Trump and other real estate developers already benefit from enormous depreciation benefits, which permit real estate developers to use paper losses (*i.e.* depreciation) to offset other earned income over time, Trump's proposals would go much farther, allowing for immediate write-offs of the expenses for new business investments, rather than over a period of years. If this were to be coupled with the current interest deduction that Mr. Trump and other real estate developers currently enjoy, both Trump and his industry colleagues would enjoy a huge windfall, virtually assuring that he would never have to pay any personal income taxes in the future.

Thus, Trump's tax proposals would only serve to increase the tax breaks for the super-rich, such as himself, if they were implemented. That is why it is important to know from Mr. Trump's existing tax returns the extent that he has benefited from past and current tax loopholes, and how much more he would benefit under his new tax plan. Of course, if his personal tax bill is now zero, it would presumably stay at zero.

Fortune has expressed some puzzlement at Trump's non-disclosure of his tax returns since his personal tax returns generally don't disclose much about an individual's business operations. A businessman's personal tax returns generally would not show any income flowing from his corporations to his personal tax returns since that corporation – assuming that they are "C-corporations," would have filed separate 1120 tax forms with the IRS. Trump, for example, listed almost 100 affiliated businesses on his filings with the Federal Election Commission.

The mere fact that these companies file separate tax returns would only create a problem for Trump if the business owner (in this case Trump) were abusing the tax laws If he used those businesses to pay for his personal expenses, such as expenses for personal residences, vacation trips, parties, golf fees, etc, that would not be legitimate business expenses. Remember, Trump has multiple homes, including a vacation home at Mar-A-Lago. He also has a Boeing 757 that he uses for both business and pleasure, and he owns about one dozen golf courses in the U.S. and Europe.

If Trump has been using any of his businesses to pay for his personal expenses, then he has a problem. As *Fortune*, in its August 5, 2016 article, reminded us, Leona Helmsley, another Manhattan real estate billionaire, "went to jail in 1989 for billing renovation on her weekend home to her company, and failing to pay taxes on the benefits."[9]

On August 31, 2016, *Business Insider* reported that billionaire businessman Mark Cuban had a different theory as to what Trump was hiding on his tax returns, and why he would not release them. [10]Cuban took a close look at a 2013 deposition from Trump, which had been uploaded to the *Washington Post* website, where Trump had disclosed that he had set up single-use subchapter S corporations for the development of his properties in Las Vegas and Chicago. As Cuban pointed out, with S-corporations (rather than C-corporations) "the entire financial performance of his company becomes part of his [personal] tax returns," since the income and losses of the businesses and corporations would "flow through to his individual tax returns.

If this is the case, namely, that Trump has primarily used S-corporation structures for his real estate development projects, then his personal tax returns would reveal much more of his entire financial picture. Moreover, since "pass-through" income is now being taxed at a ceiling of 39.6%, Trump's plan of reducing the tax rate for this income to 15% would reap him an incredible tax break bonanza.

These are only a few of the reasons why the American people are entitled to know what is contained in Mr. Trump's tax returns.

TRUMP AND HIS BUSINESSES

Much of Donald Trump's "sale's pitch" to the American public is: I am rich. I am an extremely successful businessman. Make me the CEO of the country and I will turn it around and make it successful, the same as I have done for my many businesses.

But as financial reporter Neil Barsky noted in an opinion piece for the *New York Times* on August 5, 2016, Trump's image as a successful businessman is largely a myth. "In reality, Mr. Trump was a walking disaster as a businessman for much of his life," wrote Barsky.

As Barsky describes the young Donald Trump, he "was a glamorous New York City personality and an Olympic-level self-promoter who had persuaded banks and bondholders to extend him billions of dollars of credit to buy everything from a yacht to the Plaza Hotel to the Eastern Air Lines Shuttle." Trump was indeed flying high, but when the debt he was amassing became unsustainable, he was forced quickly back to ground.[1]

Liz Mair detailed in the *Independent Journal Review* Trump's track record of piling up his businesses with unsustainable debt and then having them file for bankruptcy.[2] *CNN Money* concluded that "no major US company has filed for Chapter 11 more than Trump's casino empire in the last 30 years."[3]

Just a few years ago, Trump's company missed a huge $53.1 million bond interest payment. And as Mair explained, Trump's claim that his four business bankruptcies were all just smart corporate maneuverings ring hollow, especially since he was required to take an enormous personal hit in these bankruptcy proceedings, which required him to divest himself of a substantial portion of his shareholdings, plus yachts and airlines.

Barsky, who covered Trump from 1985 to 1991, working mainly for *The Daily News* and *The Wall Street Journal*, questioned the ability of Trump's newly opened Trump Taj Mahal Atlantic City casino to make the interest payments on its bonds. In the article, he quoted an analyst, saying, "Once the cold winds blow from October to February, it won't make it." Mr. Trump complained to the analyst's employer, and within days, the analyst was fired. But his prediction turned out to be correct.

In April 1990, Trump sent Barsky a letter from Trump's accounting firm, trying to convince Barsky of his financial strength. Oddly, however, the letter contained only information as to Trump's assets, saying that he had close to $400 million in cash and cash equivalents while omitting any information on Trump's liabilities. As any introductory Business 101 course will explain, no financial picture is complete unless it contains information on both assets and liabilities, which are the two essential ingredients for determining a person's net worth. Soon after sending this letter, Barsky reports that Trump was fighting again for his financial survival by negotiating a lifeline with his bankers.

As. explained by S.V. Date in the *National Journal,* Trump so badly mismanaged his businesses that he would have been much better off financially if he had simply invested his inheritance from his father in an S&P 500 fund. [4]

As noted in an excellent *Newsweek* article by Kurt Eichenwald published on August 12, 2016, even with the advantage of having a rich father, and thus a big head start in the business world, some of Trump's initial deals were far from successful. His first project was revitalizing the Swifton Village apartment complex in Cincinnati, which his father had purchased for $5.7 million in 1962. After Trump finished his work, they sold the complex for $6.75 million, which, while appearing to be a small return, was actually a loss.

In 1970, he took another shot at joining the entertainment business by investing $70,000, to snag a co-producer's credit for a Broadway comedy called *Paris Is Out* once again, Trump failed; the play bombed, closing after just 96 performances.

In 1972, Trump's father brought him into a limited partnership that developed and owned a senior citizen apartment complex in East Orange, New Jersey. Fred Trump also named him the beneficiary of a $1 million trust that provided him with $1.3 million in income (2015 dollars) over the next five years. In 1978, Fred Trump hired him as a consultant to help sell his ownership interest in a real estate partnership with the Grandcor Company and Port Electric Supply Corp. Although these projects were reasonably successful, they were all primarily gifts and handouts from his father.

Eventually, as detailed in Eichenwald's *Newsweek* article, through a wholly owned corporation called Wembly Realty, Trump entered into a partnership with a subsidiary of Hyatt Hotels. That company, Regency

Lexington, purchased the struggling Commodore Hotel in midtown Manhattan for redevelopment into the Grand Hyatt New York. The success of this deal depended largely on the fact that Fred Trump co-guaranteed with Hyatt a construction loan for $70 million and arranged a credit line for his son with Chase Manhattan Bank. The credit line was clearly a favor to the Trump family, which had brought huge profits to the bank. Based largely on Fred Trump's relationship with New York City politicians, the City also tossed in a 40-year tax abatement. The *Newsweek* article concluded that Trump's "success" with the Hyatt project was largely the result of money from his father, his father's bank, Hyatt and the taxpayers of New York City.

Trump's personal finances during this time period were a disaster. In 1978, the year his father obtained a credit line for him at Chase, Trump's tax returns showed personal losses of $406,386, which, according to *Newsweek,* would be $1.5 million in present-day dollars. Things got worse in 1979 when he reported an income of negative $3.4 million, or $11.2 million in today's dollars. All of this traced back to significant losses in three real estate partnerships and interest he owed Chase. Trump turned to his father once again, who in 1980 agreed to lend him $7.5 million.[5]

According to *Newsweek's* analysis, if Trump's father had not been there to repeatedly bail him out, he would have had to declare personal bankruptcy by the age of 35.

Trump decided to enter the casino business in August 1980, when he incorporated the Trump Plaza Corporation in New Jersey. Nine months later it applied for a New Jersey casino license. He formed a partnership with Harrah's Entertainment, which put up all the money in exchange for Trump developing the property. In 1984, Harrah's at Trump Plaza opened. He then purchased the nearly completed Hilton Atlantic City Hotel for just $320 million, renaming it "Trump Castle". As explained in *Newsweek*, Trump was now operating two businesses in direct competition with each other in Atlantic City, a prescription for disaster.

Trump's third casino in Atlantic City was the Taj Mahal. Since no bank or other financial institution would give him any money for the project, he financed the deal with $675 million in junk bonds, agreeing to pay an extremely high 14 percent interest, about 50 percent more than he had projected. According to *Newsweek*, that pushed Trump's total debt for his three casinos to $1.2 billion. For the renamed Trump Taj Mahal to break even, it would have to pull in as much as $1.3 million a day in revenue, more than any casino ever. Predictably, disaster struck. Most of the customers from Trump Castle and Trump Plaza moved down the Atlantic City boardwalk to the Taj Mahal. In just one year, revenues for the two smaller casinos plummeted a combined $58 million.

Trump also bought the struggling Eastern Air Lines shuttle, linking Boston, New York and Washington, D.C., and renamed it the Trump Shuttle. According to *Newsweek*, he promised to transform it into a luxury shuttle and spent $1 million to update each of the planes. But as with the casino business, Trump was taking a big gamble on a business that he knew nothing about. It turned out that customers were more interested in reliability and competitive prices, not a luxury. But the

Trump Shuttle never turned a profit, and he was eventually forced to unload it.

By June of 1990, according to *Newsweek*, Trump was on the verge of missing a $43 million interest payment on the Taj Mahal junk bonds. Believing that they had not much of alternative other than to bail him out, the banks agreed to lend him tens of millions more but insisted that Trump temporarily gives up control over all his business interests. In August 1990, New Jersey regulators prepared a report totaling Trump's debt at $3.4 billion, writing that "a complete financial collapse of the Trump Organization was not out of the question."

By December 1990, *Newsweek* recounted that, when Trump was on the verge of missing an interest payment on the debt of Trump Castle, Fred Trump came up with a certified check for $3.35 million payable to the Trump Castle. The check was deposited into that account, and a blackjack dealer paid out $3.35 million to Fred Trump's attorney in $5,000 chips. The next day, a similar "loan" was made by wire transfer, for an additional $150,000. This surreptitious, and unreported, loan allowed Donald Trump to make that interest payment. The Trump Castle Casino later settled charges by the Casino Control Commission of violations from this unlawful transaction and paid a $65,000 penalty.

Within one year of its opening, The Taj Mahal casino declared bankruptcy, and it was soon followed by Trump's two other casinos: the Plaza and the Castle. As detailed by *Newsweek*, under the reorganization, Trump turned over half his interest in the businesses in exchange for lower rates of interest, among other things. In 2004, the reorganized holding company for all of the casinos, Trump Hotels & Casino Resorts, filed for bankruptcy, and Trump was forced to give up his position as chief executive. The name of the company was then changed to Trump Entertainment Resorts, and filed for bankruptcy in 2009, four days after Trump resigned from the board.

Newsweek has also provided details of the Trump's many smaller deals that have tanked as well. For example, in 2008, he defaulted on a $640 million construction loan for Trump International Hotel & Tower in Chicago. Trump also planned to develop a 62-story luxury hotel and apartment complex in Dubai, United Arab Emirates. But when fewer wealthy expatriates than expected showed up to buy the apartments, the project quickly folded, leaving Trump with a huge loss.

Additional Trump real estate projects listed in *Newsweek* that went bust include the Trump Hollywood, a $355 million 40-story oceanfront condominium, which was foreclosed on in 2010. Similarly, the Trump Ocean Resort Baja Mexico, a 525-unit luxury vacation home complex, collapsed financially before construction really got under way. The defrauded buyers lost their $32 million in deposits. The same fraudulent scenario played out in Fort Lauderdale, Florida, where people who thought they were buying into a Trump property lost their deposits of at least $100,000. Trump took the position that he was not responsible because he had only licensed his name. Investors in another failed Florida property, Trump Tower Tampa, put up millions in 2005, believing the building was being constructed by Trump. Instead, they discovered it was all a sham in 2007.

Beginning in 2006, *Newsweek* noted that Trump made the decision to cut back on development projects, which involved risks for which Trump was losing his appetite, and started just lending his name brand to various products and enterprises. Trump announce the formation of Trump Mortgage in 2006 and then alleged that he had nothing to do with it when it collapsed 18 months later. That same year, he opened GoTrump.com, an online travel service that never amounted to more than a vanity site; according to *Newsweek,* the URL now sends searchers straight to the Trump campaign website. Also in 2006, Trump started Trump Vodka, but within a few years, the company closed because of poor sales. In 2007, Trump Steaks was unveiled, but after two months of being primarily available for sale at Sharper Image, it too died a quiet death.

The now-infamous Trump University also imploded, leaving unhappy students and a host of lawsuits in its wake. As explained in *Newsweek*, the litigation revealed plenty of evidence that the endeavor was a scam. Particularly damning was the testimony of former employee Ronald Schnackenberg, who recalled being chastised by Trump University officials for failing to push a near-destitute couple into paying $35,000 for classes by using their disability income and a home equity loan.[6]

Given Trump's proclivities for running up his company's debts and then declaring bankruptcy, would he manage the country's finances in the same reckless manner if he were to be elected as president? Would he risk running up the national debt to new heights and then defaulting? Does he plan to outfox the Chinese by luring them into buying more and more U.S. debt and then defaulting, leaving them holding the bag? Has he given any thought to how a U.S. default on its debt would be catastrophic for the interest rates for U.S. bonds that would have to be paid in the future, and how that would affect the U.S. economy and its citizens for decades to come? Probably not.

16

TRUMP AND THE DISABLED

Trump's very public dispute with a disabled reporter started in November 2015, Trump, without any evidence to support it, asserted that Muslims in Jersey City, New Jersey celebrated the collapse of the two World Trade Center towers on September 11, 2001: "I watched when the World Trade Center came tumbling down. And I watched in Jersey City, New Jersey, where thousands and thousands of people were cheering as that building was coming down. Thousands of people were cheering."

When the media questioned the accuracy of what Trump was saying, his staff did some quick background checking and came up with an article that appeared on page 6 of the *Washington Post* on September 18, 2001, describing FBI probes in northern New Jersey in the wake of the attacks. In the 15th paragraph, it said that "law enforcement authorities detained and questioned some people who were allegedly seen celebrating the attacks and holding tailgate-style parties on rooftops while they watched the devastation on the other side of the river." There was no mention of any TV or video footage that Trump could have seen that day or any other day.

Serge Kovaleski, a disabled reporter, and co-author of the article was asked what the basis for the mention about the alleged celebrations in the article. He released the same statement to every news organization: "I certainly do not remember anyone saying that thousands or even hundreds of people were celebrating. That was not the case, as best as I can remember."

His co-author, Fredrick Kunkle, also stated to *Fact Checker* that the alleged celebrations could never be confirmed: "I specifically visited the Jersey City building and neighborhood where the celebrations were purported to have happened. But I could never verify that report."[1]

At a rally at Myrtle Beach, South Carolina on November 24, 2015, Trump unloaded on Kovaleski. He repeatedly mocked him by jerking his arms in front of his body: "Now, the poor guy, you ought to see this guy, 'Ah, I don't know what I said, I don't remember, I don't remember, maybe that's what I said.'" Trump's entire horrifying imitation of a disabled person was caught on video.

Facing a firestorm of protest from disabled groups and everyone in general, Trump tried to backtrack during a rally in Colorado Springs on. Trump claimed that he was not trying to imitate a disabled person but, rather, was imitating "somebody that was groveling." According to Trump, the reporter said he had made a mistake, and that he "was groveling, grovel, grovel, grovel."

Leaving aside the fact that Kovaleski never "changed his story" or "apologized" for making a mistake, there is no question in anyone's mind that Trump intended to imitate Kovaleski's disability. The reporter has arthrogryposis, which visibly limits the functioning of his joints, which was what Trump was imitating.

Trump also claimed he did not know Kovaleski, but the reporter closely covered Trump's troubled business dealings while he was a reporter for the *N.Y. Daily News* between 1987 and 1993. Trump and Kovaleski were together on numerous occasions, and Trump well knew what he looked like and the nature of his disability.

"Donald and I were on a first-name basis for years," Kovaleski told the *Times* in November 2015. "I've interviewed him in his office," he added. "I've talked to him at press conferences. All in all, I would say around a dozen times, I've interacted with him as a reporter while I was at *The Daily News*." In particular, as reported by the *Times*, Kovaleski covered the launch of the Trump Shuttle, spending the day with Trump in 1989 when the airline launched with typical Trump hoopla.

Kovaleski is not the only disabled person that Trump has publicly mocked. He also ridiculed columnist Charles Krauthammer, who is paralyzed from the waist down. After Krauthammer referred to Trump as a "rodeo clown", Trump could not resist firing back in July 2015. As reported by the *Daily Beast* on December 2, 2015, "I went out, I made a fortune, a big fortune, a tremendous fortune… bigger than people even understand," Trump said. "Then I get called by a guy that can't buy a pair of pants, I get called names?"

Trump's insensitivity, if not disdain, for the disabled is shared by his entire organization. As detailed by the *Daily Beast* in December 2015, his properties have been sued some times for violations of the Americans With Disabilities Act ("ADA"), including one instance where a man claimed that the buses to his Atlantic City casino were virtually impossible to access in a wheelchair.[2]

James Conlon, the plaintiff in that 2003 case, alleged that he was told on two separate occasions that there were no "buses available for use by persons who use wheelchairs who choose to leave from the Long Beach, New York departure site." The case was later settled.

In another case, as reported by the *Daily Beast*, the U.S. Department of Justice intervened because the Trump Taj Mahal was nearly inaccessible for people with disabilities. The United States Attorney's Office for the District of New Jersey conducted a compliance review of Trump's Taj Mahal casino in 2011. They found that there were numerous violations, including the fact that there were no signs indicating handicapped parking in the self-park garage; a number of bathrooms lacked proper Braille for visually impaired people; the pipes in the bathroom were not insulated to prevent harm when contacted; and the counter surfaces in the buffet were not at a proper height for individuals in wheelchairs. The Casino settled the case with the federal government, promising to make the necessary updates and corrections.

Trump's problems with the disabled extended to *The Apprentice*. In 2005, attorney James Schottel Jr., a quadriplegic, sued the producers of *The Apprentice* for discrimination against the handicapped by requiring "excellent physical" health to appear on the show.

Numerous organizations for the disabled protested Trump's demeaning treatment of the disabled reporter. Former Pennsylvania Governor Tom Ridge, the chairman of the National Organization on Disability, told the *Daily Beast*: "Considering there are 56 million Americans living with a disability, you would think a candidate for president would be looking for opportunities to highlight their remarkable contributions to society, not mock them."

When President George H. W. Bush signed the ADA into law 25 years ago, he said: "We embrace you for your abilities and for your disabilities, for our similarities and indeed for our differences."

Unfortunately, Trump just doesn't get it

17

TRUMP, PSYCHOPATHOLOGY AND THE NUCLEAR CODES

Donald Trump made the headlines once again when he told Chris Matthews of MSNBC that he would "possibly" consider using a nuclear weapon as president. When Matthews questioned him further as to the use of nuclear weapons, Trump retorted: "Then why are we making them?"

Less than a week before, in an interview with the *New York Times*, Trump suggested that Japan and South Korea should consider acquiring nuclear arms as a way of disengaging the United States from its role as a military protector. A White House spokesperson promptly called such a proposal "catastrophic."

Then, on Wednesday, July 3, 2016, Joe Scarborough, on his "Morning Joe" talk show, asked the former CIA director Michael V. Hayden, whether there were safeguards in place to ensure that if Mr. Trump "gets angry, he can't launch a nuclear weapon." Scarborough, who considers himself to be a conservative, and is a former Republican Congressman, asked the question in the context of his understanding that Trump was not "the most stable guy."

Mr. Scarborough then shared a conversation that he had with a foreign policy expert who had given Mr. Trump a national security briefing. According to Scarborough, Trump asked "three times ... about the use of nuclear weapons." Trump apparently enquired of this expert: "If we have them, why can't we use them?"

If Mr. Trump doesn't already know the answer to this question, then under no circumstances should he be given access to the nuclear codes? The world is dangerous enough already, thank you.

While most psychological professionals are cautious about diagnosing someone who they have not actually treated, or even met. Apparently Mr. Trump's psychosis is evident and easy to diagnosis. As developmental psychologist Howard Gardner, a professor at the Harvard Graduate School of Education, told *Counter News* on August 4, 2016, Donald Trump is "remarkably narcissistic."[1] Clinical psychologist Ben Michaelis concurred, finding that Mr. Trump had a "textbook narcissistic personality disorder."

The Mayo Clinic defines this illness as follows: "Narcissistic personality disorder is a mental disorder in which people have an inflated sense of their own importance, a deep need for admiration and a lack of empathy for others. But behind this mask of ultra-confidence lies a fragile self-esteem that's vulnerable to the slightest criticism." Narcissism is considered to be an extreme defense against one's own feelings of worthlessness.

Clinical psychologist George Simon told *Counter News* that Trump is "so classic that I'm archiving video clips of him to use in workshops because there's no better example of his characteristics." Simon conducts lectures and seminars on manipulative behavior exhibited by narcissists, psychopaths, and sociopaths, which he explained, are all related Anti-Social Personality Disorders."

Psychologist Dan P. McAdams wrote in a piece in *The Atlantic* that it's "almost impossible to talk about Donald Trump without using the word 'narcissism.'"[2]

As discussed in the *Counter News* article of August 4, 2016, Trump's shortage of empathy can be seen clearly by his position on topics like immigration. Instead of acknowledging that reliable data shows that most Mexican immigrants are not violent, but instead people only looking for a place where actual opportunity exists, Mr. Trump harshly generalizes that they are "criminals, drug dealers, rapists, etc." It is especially ironic that Trump would take an entirely unsympathetic position to immigrants, even undocumented ones since two of his wives were immigrants.

Similarly, Trump's vow to ban all Muslims from entering the country demonstrates his emotional blindness to the fact that the refugees he speaks of are actually seeking safety from the same murderous terrorists that he wants to keep out. His call for "ID badges" to be worn by Muslims in this country is not only illegal and morally repugnant, but the striking similarity to the requirement that Jews in Nazi Germany wear the Star of David so that they could be easily identified and isolated for persecution demonstrates just how tone deaf Trump is to the historical antecedents of his proposals.

In addition to a lack of empathy, someone, such as Trump, who is apparently suffering from a narcissistic personality disorder, has a fragile self-esteem just below a thin veneer of arrogance, and this self-esteem can be easily injured by any real or perceived form of criticism. The tendency is for the person suffering from this disorder to lash out in response to any criticism, often reacting disproportionately to the perceived criticism. Sound familiar?

When Trump thought he had been treated unfairly by Fox News host and Republican debate moderator Megyn Kelly, he responded by calling her a "bimbo" and later saying that she had "blood coming out of her eyes, blood coming out of her wherever." Kelly reacted appropriately, and in a masterful understatement, said that she "may have overestimated his anger management skills."

As quoted by *Counter News*, psychotherapist Charlotte Prozan noted: "In the first debate, he talked over people and was domineering." Trump apparently did whatever he could to demean the other candidates, including telling Carly Fiorina that he didn't like her looks. When Trump perceived that Senator John McCain was critical of him, he lashed out, taunting and demeaning McCain for having been captured in Vietnam.

In one of the most prolonged and bizarre reactions that Trump had to a relatively mild critique involved writer McKay Coppins, who wrote a profile of Trump in which he called Trump's Mar-a-Lago resort in Florida a "nice, if slightly dated, hotel." You would think that Coppins had totally trash-talked the place by Trump's reaction. As Coppins recalls, "He had tweeted about me frequently in the weeks following its publication—often at odd hours, sometimes multiple times a day—denouncing me as a "dishonest slob" and "true garbage with no credibility." He added: "For two years, Trump continued to rant about how I'm a scumbag, or a loser, or 'just another phony guy.'"

TRUMP, PSYCHOPATHOLOGY AND THE NUCLEAR CODES

Wendy Terrie Behary, the author of *Disarming the Narcissist: Surviving and Thriving with the Self-Absorbed*, was quoted by *Counter News* as saying: "Narcissists are not necessarily liars, but they are notoriously uncomfortable with the truth. The truth means the potential to feel ashamed. If all they have to show the world as a source of feeling acceptable is their success and performance, be it in business or sports or celebrity, then the risk of people seeing them fail or squander their success is so difficult to their self-esteem that they feel ashamed. We call it the narcissistic injury. They're uncomfortable with their own limitations. It's not that they're cut out to lie, it's just that they can't handle what's real."[3]

Trump's unhealthy and, indeed, borderline psychotic egotism was fully on display when he was supposed to introduce his vice-presidential candidate Mike Pence. Trump had little to say about Pence, and much to say about himself. His remarks morphed into 28 minutes of self-promotion. As David Brooks described it in *The New York Times*, "The Pence announcement was truly the strangest vice-presidential unveiling in recent political history. Ricocheting around the verbal wilds for more than twice as long as the man he was introducing, Trump even refused to remain onstage and gaze on admiringly as Pence flattered him. It was like watching a guy lose interest in a wedding when the bride appears."

Hillary Clinton may not make an ideal president, and, Lord knows, she will be coming to the Oval Office with a lot of baggage. As Jim Rutenberg noted in a *New York Times* opinion piece on August 7, 2016, "there are more 'gates' affixed to [Hillary Clinton's] last name – Travelgate, Whitewatergate, now Emailgate – than there are gates in the

Old City of Jerusalem." However, no one can seriously suggest that she is mentally unstable and not to be trusted with the nuclear codes. The same cannot be said for The Donald. So why would we ever take that kind of risk? *The Economist*'s research firm Economist Intelligence Unit ranked a Trump presidency among the top ten global risks, tied with "the rising threat of jihadi terrorism destabilizing the world economy."[4] Our children and our children's children deserve better. So do we.

18

TRUMP AND HIS WORDS

Donald Trump's free association, off-the-cuff style may have attracted many votes in the Republican primaries, creating good copy for headlines and energizing his supporters. However, as at least several commentators have pointed out, what works well for him in business and in an election season may not be the best style for a sitting President. Why? Because a President's words matter. An unguarded, on the fly comment, can cause dramatic fluctuations in financial markets and create dangerous misunderstandings and miscalculations by both friends and foes abroad. That is why after centuries of hits and misses, diplomatic communications strive to be both clear, concise and measured.

Trump's communications are now so filled with over-the-top rhetoric, bombast, and confusion, it is unlikely that he would be able to change his thought and speech patterns very dramatically if he were to find himself in the Oval Office. It is not in his DNA.

For example, in October 2015, when being interviewed by *The Hill,* Trump warned of a looming recession and stock market bubble. Referring to Federal Reserve Chairwoman Janet Yellen, Trump commented: "She's keeping the economy going, barely,"[1] he said. If such comments were coming from the President of the United States rather than a presidential candidate, it would be likely to cause an immediate and dramatic reaction in the financial markets.

TRUMP, BIGOTRY, XENOPHOBIA AND RACISM

Even before the start of his campaign, Trump blatantly appealed to the dark undercurrent of bigotry, xenophobia and racism in American society. He was one of the leading advocates of the pseudo-racist "birther" movement, which suggested that Barack Obama, the first African-American President, was illegitimate since he was supposedly not a native born American, and a secret Muslim to boot.

At the onset of his Presidential campaign, Trump broadly insulted the entire Mexican population of this country by announced that he would deport all illegal aliens from Mexico, suggesting that their ranks were filled with "murderers" and "rapists." He also proposed a ban on all Muslims from entering the country, which he later modified by saying that he would require an "extreme vetting" of all Muslims, without specifying what screening measures would be employed that were not already being used.

In a February 2016 interview on CNN, Trump initially declined to condemn former Ku Klux Klan "grand wizard" David Duke when Duke announced his support for the Trump campaign. Trump claimed that he didn't even know who Duke was, which Politifact established as a lie since there was a prior record of Trump comments regarding Duke.[1] When it became clear to Trump that he had to say something, he finally disavowed Duke, claiming that a bad earpiece was to blame for his initial response.

Similarly, when a self-described white nationalist, William Johnson, was chosen to attend the Republican National Convention as a Trump delegate, the Trump campaign, after considerable delay, said that it was "a mistake." Trump has also retweeted messages from white supremacists or Nazi sympathizers, including two from an account called @WhiteGenocideTM, which features a photo of the American Nazi Party's founder. The Daily Stormer, a neo-Nazi racist website, has formally endorsed Trump.

At a Trump rally in Louisville in March, 2016, the leader of a white nationalist group, Matthew Heimback, was seen shoving a black protester, with apparent approval from Trump.

In June 2016, Trump publicly criticized Gonzalo Curiel, the federal judge handling his Trump University case as being biased because he was of "Mexican heritage", notwithstanding the fact that he had been born in Indiana and had spent many years as a federal prosecutor investigating Mexican drug cartels, at considerable personal risk.[2] House Speaker Paul Ryan referred to Trump's comments about Judge Curiel as a "textbook definition of a racist comment."

The Trump campaign put out a Tweet criticizing Hillary Clinton as corrupt with her face superimposed on a backdrop of $100 bills and a red star resembling a Star of David, which was widely interpreted as an anti-Semitic reference. The image had originally been posted weeks earlier on a Twitter account devoted to bigoted themes.[3]

The Trump campaign virtually wrote off the black vote, even in states which he must win if he has any chance to win the Presidency. Trump turned down repeated invitations to address gatherings of black leaders, while making a series of inflammatory comments about minorities. In the last Presidential race, Mitt Romney at least got 6% of the black vote, but the Trump campaign seems to have staked all of its cards on winning an overwhelming portion of the disgruntled white man's vote. However, Trump can hopefully count on at least one black vote. At one of his rallies, apparently referring to an African-American in his entourage, he referred to a member of the audience as "my black man."

The Trump Organization has also had a long history of racism. As Nicholas Kristof reported in the New York Times on July 23, 2016, Donald Trump and his father were sued back in 1973 by the U.S. Department of Justice for having systematically discriminated against blacks in housing rentals, including discrimination against blacks in the military. Black "testers" were repeatedly told by the Trump rental office in Queens, New York that there were not vacancies available, but when white testers appeared, apartments magically became available. The same Times article disclosed that the federal investigation was informed by a former building superintendent working for the Trumps that any rental application filled out by a black person was coded with the letter "C" (for colored) so that the rental office would know to reject it.[4]

Trump and his father eventually settled the civil rights suit, but three years later, the government sued the Trumps again for continuing discrimination.

In 1989, Trump led the campaign to impose the death penalty on five black teenagers who were accused of raping a white woman jogging in Central Park. The case became notoriously known as "the Central Park jogger case." All five teenagers were later exonerated, but only after spending years in prison. They were cleared by DNA evidence and the confession of a serial rapist. When the teenagers later brought a civil rights case based upon their wrongful conviction, Trump denounced the settlement of the case as "a disgrace."

Trump's racial bias also appears to have extended to his casinos. In the 1980s, according to The New Yorker, a black former Trump casino worker was quoted as saying: "When Donald and Ivanka came to the casino, the bosses would order all the black people off the floor.... They put us all in the back."

In 1991, a book by John O'Donnell, who had been president of the Trump Plaza Hotel and Casino in Atlantic City, quoted Trump as criticizing a black accountant and saying:

> Black guys counting my money! I hate it. The only kind of people I want counting my money are short guys that wear yarmulkes every day. ... I think that the guy is lazy. And it's probably not his fault, because laziness is a trait in blacks. It really is, I believe that. It's not anything they can control. [5]

Trump has retweet a graphic suggesting that 81 percent of white murder victims are killed by blacks, when the actual figure is about 15 percent.

On August 16, 2016, NBC News reported that Trump had pledged to reject "bigotry and hatred and oppression in all its forms." But the following day, the Trump campaign conclusively proved that racism, xenophobia and bigotry were indelibly embedded in the fabric of its core beliefs.

On August 17, 2016, Trump named Stephen Bannon of Breitbart News as his new campaign chief, thereby catapulting a fringe, far right flamethrower into the middle of mainstream Republican political ideology. In order to get the full flavor of what Bannon stood for, *The Guardian*, in an article published on August 27, 2016, reported on a book signing event for Ann Coulter's new book, "*In Trump We Trust: E Pluribus Awesome!*"[6]

Coulter, the outspoken conservative commentator and writer, didn't pull any punches as to her racist and xenophobic views: "The same way virtually any immigrant to Finland makes it less white, almost any immigrant to America makes it less honest," Coulter writes in her 182-page book lauding Trump. "There's nothing Trump can do that won't be forgiven. Except change his immigration policies."

The crowd at the event would have felt perfectly comfortable at the annual convention of The Aryan Nation. "Everyone says we're a nation of immigrants but we're not," said one man, wearing a Trump T-shirt. "We're a nation of northern European immigrants. We shouldn't have to pay more just to live among our own demographic." Others agreed.

The close coordination between the Trump campaign and far-right news organizations such as Breitbart News seemed to confirm the press releases from the Clinton campaign that the far right was holding Trump hostage. "The de facto merger between Breitbart and the Trump campaign represents a landmark achievement for the 'alt-right'," Clinton said. "A fringe element has effectively taken over the Republican party. All of this adds up to something we've never seen before."

Clinton added: "This is not conservatism as we have known it. This is not Republicanism as we have known it. These are racist ideas, race-baiting ideas, anti-Muslim, anti-immigrant, anti-women, all key tenets making up the emerging racist ideology known as the alt-right."

Bannon and Breitbart News took serious exception to Clinton's characterizations of their organization, but a quick survey of the organization's recent pronouncements on race and racism in America strongly support's Clinton's claims. For example, Breitbart itself recently claimed the real fascists and racists in America, the true "hate that dares not speak its name." were the "progressive mob" that "places whites at the bottom of the racial totem pole". In other words, a Trump presidency would Make America Great Again by placing white Americans back where they "deserve" to be, *i.e.,* at the top of the pecking order of privilege.

Finally, racists can say what is on their minds and in their hearts after decades of having been constrained by "political correctness," which teaches that it is no longer acceptable to be a racist in America. In Tennessee, for example, an independent candidate for Congress thanked Trump for "loosen[ing] up the overall spectrum of political discourse". The candidate echoed the presidential campaign slogan with a billboard that read: "Make America White Again."

Now that Trump and Steve Bannon have let the dark genie of racism out of the bottle, it will be difficult – if not impossible -- to put it back. On Saturday, September 3, 2016, is an attempt to offset the increasingly racist and xenophobic tone of his campaign, Trump made a much-publicized visit to Detroit, Michigan, where he appeared at an African-American church. This had more to do with allaying the concerns by moderate white Republicans and independents about the dangerous anti-minority trajectory of the Trump campaign, and less to do with any serious hope that he can boost his support among African-Americans above the 2 percent level.

Only time will tell as to whether Trump can reverse his campaign's reputation for bigotry, racism and xenophobia, but it does not seem a good bet that this tiger will be able to change its stripes.

20

TRUMP AND THE ECONOMY

On April 2, 2016, *The Washington Post* reported that Donald Trump predicted that economic conditions in the country were so perilous that it is headed for a "very massive recession." Trump has persisted in these gloomy prognostications about the economy even in the face of generally positive economic news regarding the state of the economy.[1]

Ironically, however, Trump's economic policies would have a generally depressive effect on the economy. So if in fact things are not so good now, you can count on things getting worse if Trump is elected and he actually implements his economic policies.

According to an analysis by *Politico*, many economists agreed that Trump's core policies – from increased import tariffs to mass deportations of undocumented immigrants – would hurt the economy and especially the less educated voters who support him in the greatest numbers.

Deportation of 11 Million Undocumented Immigrants

As discussed in *The Street* on July 18, 2016, some industries – such as agriculture -- that depend heavily on cheap immigrant labor would be devastated. The Street surveyed several leading economists: "There would be an abrupt drop in farm income and a sharp rise in food prices," said John McLaren, professor of economics at the University of Virginia. Local economies in areas of the country where farming is predominant would also be hurt, since the undocumented immigrant and migrant workers would no longer be there to spend their incomes and boost the local economies.

The economies of many towns and cities would also take a hit if the undocumented immigrants located there were suddenly deported. "Immigrants, whether they are legal or illegal, always spend a portion of their earnings in the location where they have their jobs," McLaren told *The Street*. "And in a lot of our urban centers, this is actually an important part of the economy." He pointed to Postville, Iowa, where in 2008 U.S. Immigration and Customs Enforcement (ICE) raided a slaughterhouse and meat packing plant, detaining 389 undocumented workers. The strike caused most of the more than 1,000 immigrants not caught to leave the town of 2,300, devastating the local economy in the process. McLaren also told The Street that each immigrant creates 1.2 local jobs for local workers, most of which go to U.S. natives. "Obviously, those jobs would disappear if the undocumented were just yanked away," he said.

Trump's proposal to force 11 million undocumented immigrants out of the country also would be economically catastrophic, and possibly lead to depression, since the economy now is close to "full employment." This means that millions of jobs now filled by undocumented immigrants – such as restaurant, hotel, and low-end construction workers – could go unfilled, causing a severe slowdown and drop in the gross national product (GNP). Even in the unlikely event that there were enough unemployed citizen workers available to take their place, U.S. documented workers would inevitably demand –and get – higher wages for the same job, which would, in turn, increase the costs of production and generally have a negative drag on the economy.

The Impact on "the American Brand"

The deportation of 11 million people from the country would also have a profound effect on how Americans view themselves, and how the rest of the world views us. As noted by Jim Pethokoukis, a columnist and blogger at the American Enterprise Institute, a center-right think tank based on Washington, D.C. "What's the American brand after we've rounded up 11 million people and sent them packing?" he is quoted in *The Street*.

Renegotiating" Trade Deals

Trump has won a significant degree of support from working class voters by saying that he will be a tougher negotiator on trade deals than the Obama administration. But no matter how tough he is, it is likely that his policies would lead to an increase in tariffs and other trade barriers. These duties, in turn, would lead to an increase in the prices of household goods, which would have a particularly negative impact on lower-middle and middle-class voters, and could trigger a significant downturn in the economy. These increased prices would, in effect, be a tax on American consumers.

Trump's Tax Policies

Perhaps most significantly, Trump's tax plan would lead to a massive increase in the deficit and damage the economy, while giving a disproportionate benefit to the very rich.

As *Politico* reported on August 8, 2016, Trump's original tax plan would have cost $10 trillion, with proposed tax rates of 0, 10, 20 and 25 percent.[2] He then junked that plan in favor of House Speaker Paul Ryan's proposed rates of 12, 25 and 33 percent, which still sharply favors those with higher incomes. However, he left unchanged his proposal to cut the top corporate rate from 35 percent to 15 percent, which would still carry a huge price tag and lead to a dramatic increase in the deficit.

According to the Tax Policy Center, as reported by *Politico,* Trump's tax plan would reduce federal revenue by $9.5 trillion over the next decade. It would also provide an average $1.3 million tax cut for the top 0.1 percent of earners, the Tax Policy Center found.[3] Trump's steadfast support for tax breaks for the wealthy seems at odds with the views of the American public. Polls consistently show that voters favor tax hikes rather than tax cuts for the rich. It is nearly impossible for Trump to paint himself as a "populist" when his policies are sharply skewed in favor of the wealthy.

By way of contrast on taxes, Clinton proposes a relatively small increase in taxes that would be borne almost entirely by the rich. Her plan would increase revenues collected by $1.1 trillion over 10 years, according to the Tax Policy Center's modeling.

As for the national debt, Trump has insisted that he would be able to get rid of the nation's more than $19 trillion national debt "over a period of eight years." He said that economic growth he foresees as a consequence of renegotiated deals would enable the United States to pay down the debt, discounting the real possibility that a trade war would erupt and cripple the U.S. economy. Trump says that only he can accomplish this goal without any adverse consequences because of his unique "aura of personality."

The Deficit

Trump has promised that he would quickly pay down the national debt if elected President through revenues generated by an expanding economy. However, few if any reputable economists would agree with his fanciful analysis. As discussed in *Politico,* Trump's proposal to quickly pay down the national debt as impossible because it could require taking more than $2 trillion a year out of the annual $4 trillion budget to pay off holders of the debt. In the face of such an enormous deficit, creditors might begin demanding higher interest rates on U.S. bonds, causing a "debt spiral" and a likely sharp drop in stock prices.

Perhaps *Moody's Analytics* summarized Trump's economic policies the best, by announcing on June 20, 2016 that a Trump presidency would "significantly" weaken the country, driving the U.S. into a "lengthy recession" with nearly 3.5 million job losses and a 7 percent unemployment rate (up from the current 4.9%). So much for making America Great Again. More like making America poor again.[4]

21

TRUMP AND HIS DOCTOR

On December 4, 2016, Dr. Harold N. Bornstein, Donald Trump's physician, wrote a "To Whom It May Concern" letter stating: "If elected, Mr. Trump, I can state unequivocally, will be the healthiest individual ever elected to the presidency."

Curious as to what Dr. Bornstein knows about the health of all of the prior Presidents of the United States, numerous reporters tried unsuccessfully to interview him regarding his unqualified "clean bill of health" of Mr. Trump.

NBC News finally tracked down Dr. Bornstein, and in an interview that aired on Friday, August 26, 2016, state that he had written Trump's "doctor's letter" in only about five minutes, while a limousine waited impatiently outside for him to finish.

Dr. Bornstein explained: "I thought about it all day and at the end, I get rushed, and I get anxious when I get rushed. So I try to get four or five lines down as fast as possible so that they would be happy. I've got five minutes to sit right at this desk and write that letter while the driver waited for me."[1]

Dr. Bornstein's letter further reported that Trump's recent lab tests were "astonishingly excellent;" his recent examination showed "only positive results;" his strength and stamina are "extraordinary;" his cardiovascular system is "excellent;" and he has "no history" of drinking or smoking.

Journalist Kurt Eichenwald noted that the reference in the doctor's letter to only "positive results" during a recent examination is not usually a good thing, since testing "positive" generally suggests a bad result. CNN's Sanjay Gupta also raised his own questions about the letter.

The letter was also strangely incomplete and suspiciously appears to have been drafted by a non-medical professional, even Mr. Trump himself. As the New York Times noted, it "contained no details about his heart rate, respiratory rate, cholesterol level, past medications or family medical history."[2] What about Mr. Trump's past medical history of venereal disease? While this may have been the anticipated occupational disease of a self-described notorious philanderer, such already public knowledge of Trump's medical history should have at least been worthy of a passing reference in the doctor's letter. After all, this letter was something more than just an employee's justification for taking a day off; it was part of the established electoral process by which Americans chose the next Leader of the Free World.

The Washington Post artfully summed it all up in an article published on August 27, 2016: "Clearly, Trump's hyperbole is itself a disease — and it's contagious."[3] In fact, Dr. Bornstein admitted in the NBC interview that he was at least somewhat influenced by the kinds of words Trump uses. Most doctors are a bit guarded in their diagnosis and prognosis of a 70-year old hyperactive male who is perpetually sleep deprived and suffers from a textbook case of an insecure egomaniacal megalomaniac, with illusions of grandeur and frequent breaks from reality. Even to the most casual observer, Mr. Trump is hanging by the slenderest of threads, which could break at the most inopportune moments, say, when he is in the Situation Room and is called upon as President to decide how to respond to the national threat. God help us!

22

TRUMP AND THE LOUISIANA FLOODING

Over the objections of Louisiana Governor John Bel Edwards that he should not come to the state just for a photo op, Donald Trump did so anyway in August 2016.

Trump was photographed helping unload a truck of goods for a full minute, and his campaign released a statement saying that he had "donated" an entire semi-truck of goods, and made a sizable cash donation.

As with his prior representations regarding his "donations" to veterans' groups, his statements about having made a contribution to help the flood victims appeared to be equally untrue, on both counts. The truckload of goods was apparently not his, and at least as of the time that he said it, there was no evidence that he had donated any money.

David Farenthold, the Washington Post reporter who had previously broken the story about the mystery donation to veterans' groups, also uncovered this new lie from Trump. Farenthold contacted the local government of Ascension Partish, where the flooding had occurred, and asked whether Trump had in fact donated a truckload of goods. A spokesperson for the Parish replied on August 20, 2016, saying: "We don't have any info about a donation truck that came from him directly."[1]

At the same time, a Trump campaign spokesperson told Fox News that Trump had donated $100,000 to the Louisiana Flood Relief

Fund. When contacted by Farenthold, however, the Fund refused to confirm that Trump had made any such donation. When the Trump campaign was asked to supply any evidence of any donation of supplies or money for flood relief victims, reporters were met with an uncharacteristic wall of silence, at least as of the news reports as of August 22, 2016.

Once again, Trump proved that in his world, words are more important than actions, and illusion is more important than reality. This may be appropriate for a Los Vegas show by a magician, but not for a potential President. Someone may actually look behind the curtain of the Great Wizard of Oz and discover that behind all the sound and bluster is only smoke and mirrors.

23

CONCLUSION

By the end of this book, I was hoping to be able to sum up Donald Trump's political philosophy, or at least the guiding principles from which his world view and position statements spring from. I wanted to set forth a neat summary of what "Trumpism" was all about. But I cannot do so. The often conflicting positions that Trump has taken on various issues do not appear to spring from any guiding principles, worldview or philosophy. He cannot be defined as a Conservative, a Neo-Con, Social Democrat, Liberal, Progressive or any of the other political labels we like to attach to our politicians, opinion makers and "talking heads" on our news programs.

Rather, the only constant that Trump believes in is Trump himself. Trump's core supporters are not primarily drawn to him because he espouses political positions that they believe in, although many of them are no doubt attracted to the anti-Hispanic, anti-Muslim, anti-immigrant, xenophobic, racist and bigoted rhetoric he generally offers up to them as raw red meat at his rallies.

What attracts Trump's army of supporters is the man himself, the image of strength, toughness, machismo, anger, violence and crude disrespect for all accepted norms of civility and cultural sensitivity that have become engrained in our social and political discourse, at least over the past several decades. It is a cult of personality that appeals to something deep in the human psyche. It is capable of unleashing strong passions in less-educated white American males who feel disenfranchised, disrespected, forgotten, passed over and easily drawn to someone who tells them that the frustrating life predicament they are trapped in is not of their own making, and that there is an easy path to restoring them to their rightful place of privilege and respect in society.

In an opinion piece in *The Washington Post* on May 18, 2016. Robert Kagan a senior fellow at the Brookings Institution, put a name on this relatively unique type of personality cult that has manifested itself in democratic and quasi-democratic societies over the past century. The name is "Fascism."

As Kagan explains in this piece, as well as a follow-up article in *Forbes* on May 31, 2016, the "National Socialist" Nazi movement that rose to power in Germany in the 1930s, and the rise of Benito Mussolini's fascist movement in Italy during the same time period, were not political philosophies or doctrines in any commonly accepted meaning of those terms. The only consistent "philosophy" set forth by Hitler in "Mein Kampf" was that all Jews should be exterminated, the Marxists should be crushed, and the Aryan race should reign supreme throughout the world. The rest of this supposedly seminal tome of National Socialism is "light, however on economic and social policy…," as Kagan correctly notes.

Mussolini changed his political "philosophy" so many times that it became clear that he had none. At various times, as Kagan discusses in his *Forbes* article, he was a socialist, a republican, anti-clerical and an atheist, and at other times, when it suited his purposes, he was a fascist, conservative and staunch protector of the Church. It made no real difference as long as "Il Duce" held the reins of power and people followed him as he established a New World Order. Kagan favorably cites to Robert O. Paxton's book, *The Anatomy of Fascism* (2004), where Paxton wrote: "Fascist leaders made no secret of having no program. Mussolini exulted in the absence …Mussolini liked to declare that he himself was the definition of Fascism." Paxton explained in greater detail in a Slate interview published on February 10, 2016, speaking of Mussolini, but describing Trump to the "T": "The details of the program were constantly changing. They said whatever seems to suit the mood of the moment."

A contemporary equivalent of the fascistic cult of personality is "Putinism," the aura of manliness and invincibility surrounding ex-KGB officer and now President Vladimir Putin, who has a large and loyal following among the Russian populace because he is perceived to be strong in protecting and promoting Russia's interests, regardless of the cost to the Russian economy and international reputation caused by its interventionist policies in Ukraine and elsewhere, and the killing of journalists and opposition leaders who oppose his actions. No matter what the cost, Putin assures the Russian people that he will protect them from their many enemies, domestic and foreign, in this dangerous and violent world.

Donald Trump also falls squarely within this mold. He willingly and almost enthusiastically discarded his liberal social positions on abortion and other subjects in order to secure the nomination of the Republican Party. During the primary campaign, and more recently in the general election campaign, Trump has continued to change his position on a myriad of issues on a daily, and in some cases, a twice-daily basis.

THE ESSENTIAL GUIDE TO DONALD TRUMP

As MSNBC commentators have recently pointed out, there seems to be the "day" Trump, who appears on talk show interviews or, on August 31st, with the Mexican President, and talks in reasonable and measured tones about the need to have a "humane" immigration and deportation policy that causes only minimal damage to the Mexican community in the U.S. Appearing with the Mexican President, Trump also emphasized the need to promote the interests of the "Hemisphere," linking the common interests of both Mexico and the U.S. This "daytime" Trump was too polite and diplomatic to raise the subject of who would pay for his Wall, even though it has been one of the signature portions of his campaign message that Mexico will pay for the Wall (even though, as Trump suggests, the Mexicans may not be smart enough yet to realize this "fact").

Later that evening, on August 31st, Trump displayed his red-faced, bellowing and confrontational "night" persona, railing once again at a rally in Phoenix about the threats that murderers and rapists within the ranks of the undocumented immigrants in this country posed to native-born citizens, and assuring his energized supporters that Mexico was going to pay for the Wall, whether it liked it or not.

Even the way that Trump sometimes juts out his jaw when he speaks is an uncanny reminder of the bombastic manner in which Mussolini and Hitler loved to parade up and down the stage before thousands of idolizing supporters, as aptly portrayed by Charlie Chaplin in the classic film, "The Great Dictator."

Trump has been an unabashed fan of Putin, no doubt because he has successfully developed the persona of the political strongman that

CONCLUSION

Trump is still refining. Perhaps he spends his spare time watching videos of Putin in order to pick up pointers. Trump has also had complimentary things to say about former Libyan leader Omar Qaddafi and the late Saddam Hussein, who Trump praised for having known how to deal with terrorists.

Trump has also been fond of retweeting a famous Mussolini quote: "It is better to live one day as a lion than 100 years as a sheep." Unsurprisingly, Trump, with his mane of yellow-orange hair, fancies himself as the lion.

In a 1990 interview with *Playboy* magazine, Trump criticized the then-General Secretary and leader of the Soviet Union, Mikhail Gorbachev, as having permitted Russia to spin "out of control" because he was too weak. In contrast, Trump gave the Tiananmen Square confrontation in Beijing, China as an example of how a government should react to an internal challenge with a show of strength. As the *National Review* discussed in its June 20, 2016 about Trump and fascism, Trump at first told his *Playboy* interviewer that he was critical of the Chinese government's reaction because they were at first too timid and "almost blew it." In other words, when the Chines army tank initially refused to roll over a protester, Trump saw this –not as an iconic image of right prevailing over might, of lone person striking a blow for human rights, democracy and freedom – but as a failure and a weakness on the part of the Chinese. However, Trump explained in the *Playboy* interview that, in his eyes, the Chinese government eventually redeemed itself and came to its senses by smashing the protesters with an iron fist. "Then they were vicious, they were horrible, but they put it down with strength. That shows you the power of strength," Trump said.

As Robert Paxton explained during an interview published in *Slate* on February 10, 2016, the core content of Trump's stump speeches – with its excoriation of undocumented Hispanic immigrants as murders and rapists, the demonization and proposal to ban all Muslims (or at least those from countries with a history of terrorism), the portrayal of the state of the country as abysmal and declining, could have been copied by Trump verbatim from the fascist playbook written by Hitler and Mussolini. "The use of ethnic stereotypes and exploitation of fear of foreigners is directly out of a fascists' recipe book," said Paxton. He added: "'Making the country great again,' sounds exactly like the fascist movements. Concern about national decline, that was one of the most prominent emotional states evoked in fascist discourse."

Paxton also recounted that Trump's staging of his arrival for a political speech by gathering his supporters at an airplane hangar" evoked the iconic image in 1932 when Hitler arrived at an airport to declare his first election victory.

It should also be remembered that the conservative power elites of Germany and Italy gave Hitler and Mussolini their support, cynically calculating that they would be able to control them after they had served their purpose, which was to crush to leftists, the socialists, the Marxists and the labor unions. But once the genie of racist, anti-Semitic mob passions had been released, they could never be easily put back in the bottle. Only the near-total devastation of Europe during World War II could eradicate the virulent cancer of fascism.

CONCLUSION

The Republican Party has made the same Mephistophelian bargain with Trump, realizing that he is not a Republican in any true sense of where that party has traditionally stood, or even after it was more recently hijacked by ultra-conservatives and tea party enthusiasts. They have made a deal with the devil because they think that Trump can return their party to power and that they can ride on the coattails of the unfathomable rage he has tapped into.

We are left with the pathetic figure of Senator John McCain, a former presidential standard bearer of the Republican Party and former Senate "maverick," who has been personally demeaned by Trump, the draft-dodger, for having been captured and imprisoned in North Vietnam during that war. Instead of taking the courageous position of rejecting Trump and everything he stands for, McCain has literally groveled at Trump's feet, announcing that he "supports" Trump as the Republican nominee for fear that Trump's supporters will run him out of his Senate seat in Arizona on a rail. McCain will probably lose his seat anyway, thanks to Trump being at the top of the ticket, so why cannot this leader and war hero who has spoken out so eloquently on so many other important issues take a firm and courageous stand against such a demagogue and neo-fascist who presents such a clear and icpresent danger to American democracy? What is the loss of a Senate seat compared to the loss of his soul, and of his honor? This sad scenario has repeated itself time and time again as one Republican politician after another, including Congressman Paul Ryan, has fallen into line and endorsed Trump's candidacy, knowing full well that a Trump Administration would be a disaster for the country and the death knell for the Republican Party as we know it. It is already the Trump Party in everything but name only.

So there we have it. Not a pretty picture. We have a Republican candidate for the Presidency of the United States who is a neo-fascist, racist, misogynistic, Muslim-phobic, xenophobic, mentally unbalanced, egomaniacal demagogue who has such contempt for democratic principles and our democratic form of government that he has already telegraphed to his rabid followers that if he loses, it will not be because the people have expressed their will, but because the election was "stolen" from him. If he loses, don't expect any concession speech extending a congratulatory hand to the presumptive next President. Instead, expect a conspiratorial rant intended to destabilize the country to the point where the people (he hopes) will call for a strongman such as him to take power, at least until the "national emergency' is over.

I believe that American is strong enough to survive a Donald Trump. It has survived many national crises before, because its people are basically good, generous and resilient. The United States also has a unique form of government that has proven time and time again that it can survive the frailties of the electorate and blunders of its misguided leaders. As Winston Churchill once said, "Democracy is the worst form of government, except for all the others."

America will emerge from this 2016 prejudicial contest stronger than ever. Of this I am certain.

CONCLUSION

ABOUT THE AUTHOR

Kenneth F. McCallion, a graduate of Yale University and Fordham Law School, is a lawyer and writer with more than 40 years of legal experience. He was a federal and state prosecutor in New York for many years, where he handled numerous organized crime and racketeering cases involving labor unions and the construction trades. He also served as an arbitrator on major construction arbitration cases involving Manhattan real estate development projects. Ken McCallion now practices law through his own law firm, McCallion & Associates LLP, which specializes in international human rights cases, environmental law, and construction law cases. He is the author of *Shoreham and the Rise and Fall of the Nuclear Power Industry*, and is an Adjunct Professor at Cardozo Law School in Manhattan. An avid sailor, he spends as much time as possible with his family and dog "Skipper" sailing the Eastern Seaboard and New England coast. He has not yet sailed to Nova Scotia.

CHAPTER NOTES

CHAPTER 1 - TRUMP AND THE MOB

[1] "Joseph McCarthy "Debate with Welch During Senate Trials" Transcript."Joseph McCarthy "Debate with Welch During Senate Trials" Transcript. Speeches-USA, n.d. Web. <http://www.speeches-usa.com/Transcripts/joseph_mccarthy-debate.html

[2] Barrett, Wayne. *Trump: The Deals and the Downfall*. New York, NY: HarperCollins, 1992. Print.

[3] Robbins, Tom. "Trump and the Mob."*The Marshall Project*. The Marshall Project, 27 Apr. 2016. Web. <https://www.themarshallproject.org/2016/04/27/trump-and-the-mob#.V9KFwUR3V>.

[4] For more on Trump and Roy Cohen see Mahler, Jonathan, and Matt Flegenheimer. "What Donald Trump Learned From Joseph McCarthy's Right-Hand Man."*The New York Times*. The New York Times, 20 June 2016. Web. http://www.nytimes.com/2016/06/21/us/politics/donald-trump-roy-cohn.html:. Krause, Michael. "Roy Cohn: Joe McCarthy's Henchman and Donald Trump's Mentor."*POLITICO Magazine*. Politico, LLC, 8 Apr. 2016. Web. http://www.politico.com/magazine/story/2016/04/donald-trump-roy-cohn-mentor-joseph-mccarthy-213799; O'Harrow, Robert, Jr., and Shawn Boburg. "The Man Who Showed Donald Trump How to Exploit Power and Instill Fear."*Washington Post*. The Washington Post, 17 June 2016. Web. <https://www.washingtonpost.com/investigations/former-mccarthy-aide-showed-trump-how-to-exploit-power-and-draw-attention/2016/06/16/e9f44f20-2bf3-11e6-9b37-42985f6a265c_story.html>.

[5] Anastasia, George. *Blood and Honor: Inside the Scarfo Mob, the Mafia's Most Violent Family*. New York: W. Morrow, 1991. Print.

[6] Barrett, Wayne. *Trump: The Deals and the Downfall*. New York, NY: HarperCollins, 1992. Print.

[7] For more on Biff Hallaron see Rowan, Roy. *The Mafia's Bite Of The Big Apple Byzantine Building Codes and Horrendous Logistics Help the Mob Control New York City Construction -- at a Price That the Big Developers Have Been All Too Willing to Pay.* – Fortune Magazine, June 6, 1988; Raab, Selwyn. "Ex-Hotel Owner With Former Ties to Mobsters Disappears."*The New York Times*. The New York Times, 29 Oct. 1998. Web. <http://www.nytimes.com/1998/10/30/nyregion/ex-hotel-owner-with-former-ties-to-mobsters-disappears.html>.

[8] Robbins, Tom. "The Truth about Donald Trump and His Links to the Mob."*Newsweek*. Newsweek, 01 May 2016. Web. <http://www.newsweek.com/truth-about-trump-mob-454053>.This piece was originally published by The Marshall Project.

[9] Robbins, Tom. "Trump and the Mob."*The Marshall Project*. The Marshall Project, 27 Apr. 2016. Web. <https://www.themarshallproject.org/2016/04/27/trump-and-the-mob#.V9KFwUR3V>. "Only a handful of union workers from Union Local 95 were employed on the site; the vast majority were illegal Polish alien workers, who worked under inhumane conditions, and who were grossly underpaid."

[10] Hays, Constance L. "Judge Says Trump Tower Builders Cheated Union on Pension Funds."*The New York Times*. The New York Times, 26 Apr. 1991. Web. <http://www.nytimes.com/1991/04/27/nyregion/judge-says-trump-tower-builders-cheated-union-on-pension-funds.html>.

[11] Salo, Jackie. "Donald Trump's Fellow Military Academy Alums Remember School A Little Differently Than The Presidential Candidate."*International Business Times*. IBT Media, 12 Sept. 2015. Web. <http://www.ibtimes.com/donald-trumps-fellow-military-academy-alums-remember-school-little-differently-2093990>.

[12] Isikoff, Michael. "Trump Challenged over Ties to Mob-linked Gambler with Ugly past."*[Video]*. Yahoo, 7 Mar. 2016. Web. <https://www.yahoo.com/news/trump-challenged-over-ties-to-mob-linked-gambler-100050602.html>.

[13] Krueger, Katherine. "Report Raises New Questions About Trump's Ties To N.J. Mob-Linked Figure."*TPM*. N.p., 07 Mar. 2016. Web. <http://talkingpointsmemo.com/livewire/trump-robert-libutti-reported-mob-ties>.

[14] Isikoff, Michael. "Trump Challenged over Ties to Mob-linked Gambler with Ugly past."*[Video]*. Yahoo, 7 Mar. 2016. Web. <https://www.yahoo.com/news/trump-challenged-over-ties-to-mob-linked-gambler-100050602.html>.

[15] IBID

[16] IBID

[17] Coleman, Oliver, and Denis Slattery. "Sammy Gravano's Daughter Wants Dad's Pal Trump for President."*NY Daily News*. N.p., 9 Mar. 2016. Web. <http://www.nydailynews.com/news/politics/sammy-gravano-daughter-dad-pal-trump-president-article-1.2557697>.

[18] IBID

[19] Helderman, Rosalind S., and Tom Hamburger17. "Former Mafia-linked Figure Describes Association with Trump. "*Washington Post*. The Washington Post, 17 May 2016. Web. <https://www.washingtonpost.com/politics/former-mafia-linked-figure-describes-association-with-trump/2016/05/17/cec6c2c6-16d3-11e6-aa55-670cabef46e0_story.html>. Also: "Trump Describes Association with Felix Sater." *Washington Post*. The Washington Post, 17 May 2016. Web. <http://www.washingtonpost.com/video/national/trump-describes-association-with-felix-sater/2016/05/17/ccfeac7c-1c4d-11e6-82c2-a7dcb313287d_video.html>.

[20] O'Brien, Timothy L. *TrumpNation: The Art of Being the Donald*. New York: Warner Business, 2005. Print. Also: Goodman, Peter S. "Trump Suit Claiming Defamation Is Dismissed."*The New York Times*. The New

York Times, 15 July 2009. Web. 31 Aug. 2016. <http://www.nytimes.com/2009/07/16/business/media/16trump.html>.

[21] Sallah, Michael, and Michael Vasquez. "Failed Donald Trump Tower Thrust into GOP Campaign for Presidency."*Miamiherald*. N.p., 12 Mar. 2016. Web. <http://www.miamiherald.com/news/politics-government/election/article65709332.html>.

[22] "Trump: Cocaine Dealer? What Cocaine Dealer?"*The Smoking Gun*. N.p., 1 Mar. 2016. Web. 31 Aug. 2016. <http://www.thesmokinggun.com/documents/celebrity/trump-dge-report-weichselbaum-563821>. Also: Johnston, David Cay. "Just What Were Donald Trump's Ties to the Mob? "*POLITICO Magazine*. N.p., 22 May 2016. . <http://www.politico.com/magazine/story/2016/05/donald-trump-2016-mob-organized-crime-213910>.

CHAPTER 2 – TRUMP AND TORTURE

[1] Paletta, Damian. "Trump Reverses His Stance on Torture."*WSJ*. The Wall Street Journal, 4 Mar. 2016. <http://www.wsj.com/articles/trump-reverses-his-stance-on-torture-1457116559>.

[2] Benen, Steve. "Donald Trump Sees a Problem Only Torture Can Solve."*Msnbc.com*. NBC News Digital, 29 June 2016. Web. <http://www.msnbc.com/rachel-maddow-show/donald-trump-sees-problem-only-torture-can-solve>.

[3] Donald Trump sees a problem only torture can solve | MSNBC." Insert Name of Site in Italics. N.p., n.d. Web. 04 Sep. 2016 <http://www.msnbc.com/rachel-maddow-show/donald-trump-sees-problem-only-torture-c>.

[4] Kirkland, Allegra. "Trump Responds to Istanbul Suicide Bombings With New Calls For Torture." *TPM*. N.p., 29 June 2016. Web. <http://talkingpointsmemo.com/livewire/trump-responds-istanbul-waterboarding-torture>see also: "Trump on Terror: "You Have To Fight Fire With Fire ..." *www.realclearpolitics.com*. N.p., n.d. Web. 04 Sep. 2016
<http://www.realclearpolitics.com/video/2016/06/28/trump_on_terror_you_have_to_fi>.

[5] See http://www.cnn.com/TRANSCRIPTS/1603/23/cnnt.02.html

[6] Frumin, Aliyah. "McCain Hits Back at Trump on Waterboarding."*NBC News*. NBC Universal, 29 June 2016. Web. <http://www.nbcnews.com/politics/2016-election/mccain-hits-back-trump-waterboarding-n601026>.

[7] George Walker Bush, as quoted in 2002 State of the Union address (29 January 2002), Washington, D.C.

[8] "A Guide to the Memos on Torture." N.p., n.d. Web. <http://www.nytimes.com/ref/international/24MEMO-GUIDE.html>.

[9] Herbert, Bob. "The Rumsfeld Stain."*The New York Times*. The New York Times, 23 May 2005. Web. <http://www.nytimes.com/2005/05/23/opinion/the-rumsfeld-stain.html>.

[10] "Previously Secret Torture Memo Released."*CNN*. Cable News Network, 24 July 2008. Web. 31 Aug. 2016. <http://www.cnn.com/2008/POLITICS/07/24/cia.torture/index.html>.

[11] For earlier discussion on McCain and torture see: Santorum goes up against two McCains on use of torture." www.usetoday.com. N.p., n.d. <http://content.usatoday.com/communities/onpolitics/post/2011/05/john-mccain-rick>.

[12] Abramsky, Sasha. "Exactly What Kind of Torture Does Donald Trump Want to Use?"*The Nation*. N.p., 25 Mar. 2016. Web. <https://www.thenation.com/article/exactly-what-kind-of-torture-does-donald-trump-want-to-use/>.

[13] IBID

[14] IBID

[15] U.S. Department of State, "Initial Report of the United States of America to the UN Committee Against Torture." Oct 15, 1999. (15 Nov. 2001) See also: "The Legal Prohibition Against Torture | Human Rights Watch." <https://www.hrw.org/news/2003/03/11/legal-prohibition-against-torture>.

[16] IBID

[17] IBID

[18] IBID

[19] For more on torture and the law see: Marty Lederman: "GTMO: Where Was the Law? Whither the UCMJ http://www.acslaw.org/acsblog/marty-lederman-gtmo-where-was-the-law-whither-the-

[20] The Legal Prohibition Against Torture | Human Rights Watch<https://www.hrw.org/news/2003/03/11/legal-prohibition-against-torture>.

[21] IBID

[22] Thomson Reuters. "John McCain Criticizes Donald Trump's Support for Waterboarding. "*Http://www.cbc.ca/m/touch/world/story/1.3658875*. Canadian Broadcasting Company, 29 June 2016. Web. <http://www.cbc.ca/m/touch/world/story/1.3658875>.see also: "John McCain Explains to Donald Trump in Very Small Words ..." <http://wonkette.com/603617/john-mccain-explains-to-donald-trump-in-very-small-words>

[23] IBID

[24] Is torture right? | Debate.org <http://www.debate.org/opinions/is-torture-right>.

[25] Sadat, Leila Nadya., and Michael P. Scharf. *The Theory and Practice of International Criminal Law: Essays in Honor of M. Cherif Bassiouni*. Leiden: Martinus Nijhoff, 2008. Print.

CHAPTER 3 – TRUMP AND THE MUSLIMS

[1] A Full List of Donald Trump's Rapidly Changing Policy ..."
http://www.nbcnews.com/politics/2016-election/full-list-donald-trump-s-rapidly-changing-policy-positions>

[2] Timm, Jane. "Here Are All of Donald Trump's Flip-flops on Big Issues." *NBC News*. NBC Universal, 30 Aug. 2016. Web.
<http://www.nbcnews.com/politics/2016-election/full-list-donald-trumps-rapidly-changing-policy-positions-n547801>.

[3] See Michael Hayden: Trump Is Helping ISIS - huffingtonpost.com
<http://www.huffingtonpost.com/entry/michael-hayden-donald-trump-isis_us_574c46f1>.

[4] Trump's Ban on Muslims Is Unconstitutional and Obscures
<http://www.huffingtonpost.com/ivan-eland/trumps-ban-on-muslims-is_b_8804284.html>.

[5] Dad of slain Muslim soldier challenges Trump - yahoo.com
<https://www.yahoo.com/news/dad-slain-muslim-soldier-challenges-trump-023308372.h>.

[6] Trump faces backlash over attacks on family of slain ..."
<http://www.cnn.com/2016/07/31/politics/donald-trump-khizr-khan-family-controvers>.

[7] Trump reignites Khan feud, says father? viciously attacked ..."
<http://www.politico.com/story/2016/08/trump-khan-feud-226494>.

[8] Khan, Ghazala. "Ghazala Khan: Trump Criticized My Silence. He Knows Nothing about True Sacrifice. "*Washington Post*. The Washington Post, 31 July 2016. Web.
<https://www.washingtonpost.com/opinions/ghazala-khan-donald-trump-criticized-my-silence-he-knows-nothing-about-true-sacrifice/2016/07/31/c46e52ec-571c-11e6-831d-0324760ca856_story.html>.

[9] Bradner, Eric. "Did Trump Go Too Far?" *CNN*. Cable News Network, 1 Aug. 2016. Web. <http://www.cnn.com/2016/07/31/politics/donald-trump-khizr-khan-family-controversy/index.html>.

[10] Wright, David. "While Khan Talks Peace, Trump Tweets against Him."*CNN*. Cable News Network, 1 Aug. 2016. Web. <http://www.cnn.com/2016/08/01/politics/khans-donald-trump-cnn-new-day/index.html>.Also: Trump faces backlash over attacks on family of slain ..." <http://www.cnn.com/2016/07/31/politics/donald-trump-khizr-khan-family-controvers>.

CHAPTER 4 – TRUMP AND THE CHRISTIANS

[1] Falwell, Jerry, Jr. "Jerry Falwell Jr.: Trump Is the Churchillian Leader We Need." *Washington Post*. The Washington Post, 19 Aug. 2016. Web. <https://www.washingtonpost.com/opinions/jerry-falwell-jr-trump-is-the-churchillian-leader-we-need/2016/08/19/b1ff79e0-64b1-11e6-be4e-23fc4d4d12b4_story.html>.

[2] Wehner, Peter. "Under the Dark Spell of Trump, Jerry Falwell Jr. Is Damaging Public Christian Witness."*National Review*. The National Review, 25 Aug. 2016. Web. <http://www.nationalreview.com/article/439326/erry-falwell-jr-donald-trumps-flatterer-pushing-christ-rear>.

[3] IBID

[4] IBID

CHAPTER 5 – TRUMP AND JEWS

[1] Dillon, Nancy. "Trump Campaign CEO Bannon Complained of Jews at Daughters' School."*NY Daily News*. N.p., 27 Aug. 2016. Web. <http://www.nydailynews.com/news/election/trump-campaign-ceo-bannon-complained-jews-daughters-school-article-1.2767615>.

[2] Politi, Daniel. "Trump Tweets (Then Deletes) Image of Clinton, a Pile of Money, and Star of David." *Slate Magazine*. N.p., 02 July 2016. Web. <http://www.slate.com/blogs/the_slatest/2016/07/02/trump_tweets_image_of_clinton_a_pile_of_money_and_star_of_david.html>.

[3] Easley, Jonathan. "Jewish Voters Could Tip Swing States Hillary Clinton's Way."*TheHill*. N.p., 06 July 2016. Web. <http://thehill.com/homenews/campaign/286583-jewish-voters-could-tip-swing-states-hillary-clintons-way>.

[4] Shalev, Chemi, and 17.07.2016 | 22:08 14 Comments. "Trump's Candidacy and the GOP Platform Are as Much Anti-Jewish as 'pro-Israeli'" *Trump's Candidacy and the GOP Platform Are as Much Anti-Jewish as 'pro-Israeli'*N.p., 17 July 2016. Web. <http://www.haaretz.com/wwwMobileSite/world-news/u-s-election-2016/1.731381?v=7AD9A2EF0BFA01DF2BA75775B578CF5A>.

[5] IBID

[6] IBID

[7] IBID

CHAPTER 6 – TRUMP AND WOMEN

[1] Cohen, Claire. "Donald Trump Sexism Tracker: Every Offensive Comment in One Place." **The Telegraph** Telegraph Media Group, 4 June 2016. Web. <http://www.telegraph.co.uk/women/politics/donald-trump-sexism-tracker-every-offensive-comment-in-one-place/>

[2] "Trump: If Abortions Are Banned, Women Who Seek Them Should Face 'punishment'. "*Washington Post*. The Washington Post. <https://www.washingtonpost.com/news/post-politics/wp/2016/03/30/trump-if-abortions-were-banned-women-who-seek-them-would-face-punishment/>.

[3] Brenner, Marie. "After The Gold Rush." *Vanity Fair*. N.p., 01 Sept. 1990. Web. <http://www.vanityfair.com/magazine/2015/07/donald-ivana-trump-divorce-prenup-marie-brenner>.

[4] Rappeport, Alan. "Donald Trump's Trail of Comments About Women."*The New York Times*. The New York Times, 25 Mar. 2016. Web. <http://www.nytimes.com/2016/03/26/us/politics/donald-trump-women.html>.

[5] Shire, Emily. *The Daily Beast*. Newsweek/Daily Beast, 7 Aug. 2015. Web. 04 Sept. 2016. <http://www.thedailybeast.com/articles/2015/08/07/he-said-she-said-donald-trump-vs-rosie-o-donnell.html>.

[6] Maddux, Mitchel. "Fired Losers Lash 'sexist' Trump."*New York Post Fired Losers Lash Sexist Trump Comments*. N.p., 02 Nov. 2010. Web. <http://nypost.com/2010/11/02/fired-losers-lash-sexist-trump/>.

[7] Diamond, Jeremy. "Trump Calls Lawyer 'disgusting' for Going to Pump Breast Milk, Report Says." *CNN*. Cable News Network, 29 July 2015. Web. <http://www.cnn.com/2015/07/29/politics/trump-breast-pump-statement/index.html>.

[8] Reporter, Daily Mail. "'No Wonder Your Husband Left You for a Man': Donald Trump Wages War on Arianna Huffington with Acidic Tweets." *Mail Online*. Associated Newspapers, 30 Aug. 2012. Web. <http://www.dailymail.co.uk/news/article-2195045/Donald-Trump-wages-Twitter-war-Arianna-Huffington-No-wonder-husband-left-man.html>.

[9] Prejean, Carrie. *Still Standing: The Untold Story of My Fight against Gossip, Hate, and Political Attacks*. Washington, D.C.: Regnery Pub., 2009. Print

[10] Viser, Matt. "The Pageant of Donald Trump's Dreams - The Boston Globe."*BostonGlobe.com*. N.p., 17 Apr. 2016. Web. <https://www.bostonglobe.com/news/politics/2016/04/16/trump/P6jVWXAzaG12Ou5dPXYCDL/story.html>.

[11] Graham, David A. "The Many Scandals of Donald Trump: A Cheat Sheet."*The Atlantic*. Atlantic Media Company, 30 Aug. 2016. Web. http://www.theatlantic.com/politics/archive/2016/08/donald-trump-scandals/474726/

[12] Rucker, Phil. "Trump Says Fox's Megyn Kelly Had 'blood Coming out of Her Wherever'." *Washington Post*. The Washington Post, 8 Aug. 2015. Web. <https://www.washingtonpost.com/news/post-politics/wp/2015/08/07/trump-says-foxs-megyn-kelly-had-blood-coming-out-of-her-wherever/>.

[13] Viser, Matt. "Boston Globe: Trump Campaign Pays Women Less Than Men."*Newsmax*. N.p., 06 June 2016. Web. <http://www.newsmax.com/Politics/income-gap-wages-campaign-staff-donald-trump/2016/06/06/id/732532/>.

[14] Mirkinson, Jack. "Donald Trump's Awful Tweet About Sexual Assault In The Military." *The Huffington Post*. TheHuffingtonPost.com, 8 May 2013. Web. <http://www.huffingtonpost.com/2013/05/08/donald-trump-tweet-sexual-assault-military_n_3239781.html>.

CHAPTER 7 - TRUMP AND THE WALL

[1] A Full List of Donald Trump's Rapidly Changing Policy <http://www.nbcnews.com/politics/2016-election/full-list-donald-trumps-rapidly-c>.

[2] "Here's Another Reason Not to Support Trump's Border Wall." <http://gizmodo.com/heres-another-reason-not-to-support-trumps-border-wall-178543>.

[3] IBID

[4] IBID Also: "News and Research Communications." *U.S.-Mexico Border Wall Could Threaten Wildlife Species, Biologists Warn*. Oregon State University, 7 July 2009. Web. <http://oregonstate.edu/ua/ncs/archives/2009/jul/us-mexico-border-wall-could-threaten-wildlife-species-biologists-warn>.

[5] IBID

[6] "Donald Trump, Wavering on Immigration, Finds Anger in All ..." <http://www.nytimes.com/2016/08/26/us/politics/donald-trump-immigration.htm

[7] IBID

[8] Coulter, Ann H. *In Trump We Trust: How He Outsmarted the Politicians, the Elites and the Media*. London: Biteback, 2016. Print.

[9] Former Trump Models: We Were Told to Lie About Immigration ..."
<http://www.thedailybeast.com/cheats/2016/08/30/ex-trump-models-recall-sweatshop->.

[10] IBID

[11] West, James. "Former Models for Donald Trump's Agency Say They Violated Immigration Rules and Worked Illegally."*Mother Jones*. N.p., 30 Aug. 2016. Web.
<http://www.motherjones.com/politics/2016/08/donald-trump-model-management-illegal-immigration>.

[12] IBID

[13] IBID

[14] "Donald Trump's history of using undocumented immigrant ..." <http://www.slate.com/blogs/the_slatest/2016/08/30/>

[15] IBID

[16] Bagli, Charles V., and Megan Twohey. "Donald Trump to Foreign Workers for Florida Club: You're Hired."*The New York Times*. The New York Times, 25 Feb. 2016. Web.
<http://www.nytimes.com/2016/02/26/us/politics/donald-trump-taps-foreign-work-force-for-his-florida-club.html>.

[17] IBID

[18] Trump Recommits to Mass Deportation in Fiery Immigration <http://www.nbcnews.com/politics/2016-election/trump-recommits-mass-deportation-f>.

[19] IBID

[20] "Just how many people would Trump deport? - yahoo.com." <https://www.yahoo.com/news/m/08faef10-a5df-3b17-bd08-1d42ff90f543/ss_just-how-ma>.

[21]Todd, Chuck, First Read Trump Recommits to Mass Deportation in Fiery Immigration http://www.nbcnews.com/politics/2016-election/trump-recommits-mass-deportation-f

CHAPTER 8-TRUMP AND THE RUSSIANS

[1] Myers, Steven Lee, and Andrew E. Kramer. "How Paul Manafort Wielded Power in Ukraine Before Advising Donald Trump." *The New York Times*. The New York Times, 31 July 2016. Web. <http://www.nytimes.com/2016/08/01/us/paul-manafort-ukraine-donald-trump.html>. Also: Burns, Alexander, and Maggie Haberman. "Mystery Man: Ukraine's U.S. Fixer."*POLITICO*. N.p., 5 Mar. 2014. Web. <http://www.politico.com/story/2014/03/paul-manafort-ukraine-104263>.

[2] Woodruff, Betsy, and Tim Mark. "BLOOD MONEY Top Trump Aide Led the 'Torturers' Lobby'." *The Daily Beast*. Newsweek/Daily Beast, 13 Apr. 2016. Web. http://www.thedailybeast.com/articles/2016/04/13/top-trump-aide-led-the-torturers-lobby.html

[3] Foer, Franklin. "If You Don't Think Paul Manafort Can Get Trump Elected, You Don't Know Paul Manafort." *Slate Magazine*. N.p., 28 Apr. 2016. Web. <http://www.slate.com/articles/news_and_politics/politics/2016/04/paul_manafort_isn_t_a_gop_retread_he_s_made_a_career_of_reinventing_tyrants.html

[4] James, Joy, *Resisting State Violence: Radicalism, Gender, and Race in U.S. Culture*. Minneapolis, MN: U of Minnesota, 1996. Print.

[5] Brogan, Pamela. "The Torturers' Lobby. "*The Torturer's Lobby* (n.d.): n. pag..*publicintegrity.org/legacy_projects/pdf_reports/THETORTURERSLOBBY.pdf*. The Center for Public Integrity. Web.

[6] IBID

[7] Woodruff, Betsy, and Tim Mark. "BLOOD MONEY Top Trump Aide Led the 'Torturers' Lobby'." *The Daily Beast*. Newsweek/Daily Beast, 13

Apr. 2016. Web. http://www.thedailybeast.com/articles/2016/04/13/top-trump-aide-led-the-torturers-lobby.html

[8] Delios, Hugh. "Victims Describe Mobutu's Long Reign Of Torture."*Tribunedigital-chicagotribune*. The Chicago Tribune, 29 Apr. 1997. Web. <http://articles.chicagotribune.com/1997-04-29/news/9704290128_1_president-mobutu-sese-seko-secret-detention-centers-laurent-kabila>.

[9] Vogel, Kenneth P. "Paul Manafort's Wild and Lucrative Philippine Adventure." *POLITICO Magazine*. Politico.com, 10 June 2016. Web. <http://www.politico.com/magazine/story/2016/06/2016-donald-trump-paul-manafort-ferinand-marcos-philippines-1980s-213952>.

[10] Natta, Don Van, and Douglas Frantz. "Lobbyists Are Friends and Foes to McCain."*The New York Times*. The New York Times, 09 Feb. 2000. Web. <http://www.nytimes.com/2000/02/10/us/2000-campaign-special-interests-money-lobbyists-are-friends-foes-mccain.html>.

[12] Stone, Peter. "Trump's New Right-hand Man Has History of Controversial Clients and Deals. "*The Guardian*. Guardian News and Media, 27 Apr. 2016. Web. <https://www.theguardian.com/us-news/2016/apr/27/paul-manafort-donald-trump-campaign-past-clients>.

[13] Kramer, Andrew E., Mike McIntire, and Barry Meier. "Secret Ledger in Ukraine Lists Cash for Donald Trump's Campaign Chief." *The New York Times*. The New York Times, 14 Aug. 2016. Web. <http://www.nytimes.com/2016/08/15/us/politics/paul-manafort-ukraine-donald-trump.html>.

[14] IBID

[15] Horwitz, Jeff and Desmond Butler, "AP Sources: Manafort Tied to Undisclosed Foreign Lobbying." *The Big Story*. Associated Press, 17 Aug. 2016. Web. <http://bigstory.ap.org/article/c01989a47ee5421593ba1b301ec07813/ap-sources-manafort-tied-undisclosed-foreign-lobbying>.

[16] IBID

[17] Mufson, Steven, and Tom Hamburger. "Inside Trump Adviser Manafort's World of Politics and Global Financial Dealmaking." *Washington Post*. The Washington Post, 26 Apr. 2016. Web. <https://www.washingtonpost.com/politics/in-business-as-in-politics-trump-adviser-no-stranger-to-controversial-figures/2016/04/26/970db232-08c7-11e6-b283-e79d81c63c1b_story.html>.

[18] Hamburger, Tom, Dana Priest, and Andrew Roth. "How Trump Adviser Manafort Revived His Career - and Business Fortunes - in Ukraine." *Washington Post*. The Washington Post, 18 Aug. 2016. Web. <https://www.washingtonpost.com/politics/how-trump-adviser-manafort-revived-his-career--and-business-fortunes--in-ukraine/2016/08/18/8bcfb144-648f-11e6-be4e-23fc4d4d12b4_story.html>.

[19] Mak, Tim, and Alexa Corse. "Trump Campaign Changed Ukraine Platform, Lied About It." *The Daily Beast*. Newsweek/Daily Beast, 3 Aug. 2016. Web. <http://www.thedailybeast.com/articles/2016/08/03/trump-campaign-changed-ukraine-platform-lied-about-it.html>.

[20] IBID

[21] IBID

[22] IBID

[23] Priest, Dana, and Greg Miller. "He Was One of the Most Respected Intel Officers of His Generation. Now He's Leading 'Lock Her Up' Chants." *Washington Post*. The Washington Post, 15 Aug. 2016. Web. 05 Sept. 2016. <https://www.washingtonpost.com/world/national-security/nearly-the-entire-national-security-establishment-has-rejected-trumpexcept-for-this-man/2016/08/15/d5072d96-5e4b-11e6-8e45-477372e89d78_story.html>.

[24] IBID

[25] Mufson, Steven, and Tom Hamburger. "Trump Adviser's Public Comments, Ties to Moscow Stir Unease in Both Parties."*Washington

Post. The Washington Post, 5 Aug. 2016. Web.
<https://www.washingtonpost.com/business/economy/trump-advisers-public-comments-ties-to-moscow-stir-unease-in-both-parties/2016/08/05/2e8722fa-5815-11e6-9aee-8075993d73a2_story.html>.

[26] Mider, Zachery. "Trump Russia Adviser Carter Page Interview."*Bloomberg.com*. Bloomberg, 30 Mar. 2016. Web. <http://www.bloomberg.com/politics/articles/2016-03-30/trump-russia-adviser-carter-page-interview>.

[27] IBID

[28] @hrw. "2015." *Human Rights Watch*. N.p., 29 June 2015. Web. <https://www.hrw.org/world-report/2015>.

CHAPTER 9 - TRUMP AND HIS TEAM

[1] *CNN*. Cable News Network, 12 Aug. 2016. Web. <http://www.cnn.com/TRANSCRIPTS/1608/12/cnr.05.html>.

[2] Hananoki, Eric. "A Comprehensive Guide to Trump Ally Roger Stone, A Racist, Sexist Conspiracy Theorist." *Media Matters for America*. N.p., 09 May 2016. Web. <http://mediamatters.org/research/2016/05/09/comprehensive-guide-trump-ally-roger-stone-racist-sexist-conspiracy-theorist/210303>.

[3] Rucker, Phillip, and Robert Costa. "While the GOP Worries about Convention Chaos, Trump Pushes for 'showbiz' Feel."*Washington Post*. The Washington Post, 17 Apr. 2016. Web. <https://www.washingtonpost.com/politics/while-the-gop-worries-about-convention-chaos-trump-pushes-for-showbiz-feel/2016/04/17/482cc914-0322-11e6-9d36-33d198ea26c5_story.html>.

[4] Hillman, Jesse. "Politics." *Roger Stone: If Clinton Wins, I'm Moving to Costa Rica*. N.p., 27 Aug. 2016. Web. <http://www.gamefaqs.com/boards/261-politics/74217578?page=1>.

CHAPTER 10 – TRUMP AND THE SECOND AMENDMENT PEOPLE

[1] LoBianco, Thomas. "Reagan Daughter Blasts Trump for Inciting Violence."*CNN*. Cable News Network, 11 Aug. 2016. Web. <http://www.cnn.com/2016/08/11/politics/reagan-daughter-blasts-trump/index.html>.

[2] Friedman, Thomas L. "Trump's Wink Wink to 'Second Amendment People'."*The New York Times*. The New York Times, 09 Aug. 2016. Web. <http://www.nytimes.com/2016/08/10/opinion/trumps-ambiguous-wink-wink-to-second-amendment-people.html>.

CHAPTER 11 TRUMP AND GUNS

[1] Savransky, Rebecca. "Trump: If Clubgoers Had Guns, Orlando Tragedy Wouldn't Have Been as Bad."*TheHill*. N.p., 13 June 2016. Web. <http://thehill.com/blogs/ballot-box/presidential-races/283234-trump-if-you-had-guns-in-the-club-you-wouldnt-have-had>.

[2] Prynce, Darc. "Howie Carr: Donald Trump Interview (06/13/16)." *YouTube*. YouTube, 13 June 2016. Web. https://www.youtube.com/watch?v=0fSXtMdEmVc

CHAPTER 12 – TRUMP AND VETERANS

[1] Fahrenhold, David A. "What We Know — and What We Don't — about the Money Donald Trump Raised for Veterans."*Washington Post*. The Washington Post, 24 May 2016. Web. <https://www.washingtonpost.com/news/post-politics/wp/2016/05/24/what-we-know-and-what-we-dont-about-the-money-donald-trump-raised-for-veterans/>.

CHAPTER 13 – TRUMP AND THE ELECTORAL SYSTEM

[1] Sullivan, Sean. "Trump Urges Pennsylvania Backers: Don't Just Vote, Watch for Signs of 'cheating' on Election Day." *Washington Post*. The Washington Post, 12 Aug. 2016. Web. https://www.washingtonpost.com/news/post-politics/wp/2016/08/12/trump-urges-pennsylvania-backers-dont-just-vote-watch-for-signs-of-cheating-on-election-day/

² "Donald Trump Cues Up Another Conspiracy." *The New York Times*. The New York Times, 22 Aug. 2016. Web. <http://www.nytimes.com/2016/08/23/opinion/donald-trump-cues-up-another-conspiracy.html>.

CHAPTER 14 – TRUMP AND TAXES

¹ Zuckoff, Mitchell. "Why We Ask to See Candidates' Tax Returns."*The New York Times*. The New York Times, 05 Aug. 2016. Web. <http://www.nytimes.com/2016/08/06/opinion/why-we-ask-to-see-candidates-tax-returns.html>.

² Richter, Greg. "Trump: Romney Might Have Lost for Releasing Taxes."*Newsmax*. N.p., 28 July 2016. Web. <http://www.newsmax.com/Politics/donald-trump-tax-returns-irs-mitt-romney/2016/07/28/id/741111/>.

³ Fahrenthold, David. "Trump Promised Millions to Charity. We Found Less than $10,000 over 7 Years."*Washington Post*. The Washington Post, 28 June 2016. Web. <https://www.washingtonpost.com/politics/trump-promised-millions-to-charity-we-found-less-than-10000-over-7-years/2016/06/28/cbab5d1a-37dd-11e6-8f7c-d4c723a2becb_story.html>.

⁴ Santucci, John, and Veronica Stracqualursi. "Donald Trump Refuses to Reveal His Tax Rate: 'It's None of Your Business" *ABC News*. ABC News Network, 13 May 2016. Web. http://abcnews.go.com/Politics/donald-trump-refuses-reveal-tax-rate-business/story?id=39086788

⁵ Harwell, Drew. "Trump Once Revealed His Income Tax Returns. They Showed He Didn't Pay a Cent." *Washington Post*. The Washington Post, 21 May 2016. Web. <https://www.washingtonpost.com/politics/trumps-income-tax-returns-once-became-public-they-showed-he-didnt-pay-a-cent/2016/05/20/ffa2f63c-1b7c-11e6-b6e0-c53b7ef63b45_story.html>.

⁶ Goldmacher, Shane. "Trump Appears to Have Paid No Taxes for Two Years in Early 1990s."*POLITICO*. N.p., 17 June 2016. Web. <http://www.politico.com/story/2016/06/donald-trump-no-taxes-224498>.

[7] Stewart, James G. "If Trump Gets His Way, Real Estate Will Get Even More Tax Breaks." *The New York Times*. The New York Times, 01 Sept. 2016. Web. <http://www.nytimes.com/2016/09/02/business/economy/if-trump-gets-his-way-real-estate-will-get-even-more-tax-breaks.html>.

[8] IBID

[9] Tully, Shawn. "5 Things You Need to Know About Donald Trump's Tax Returns." *Fortune 5 Things You Need to Know About Donald Trumps Tax Returns Comments*. N.p., 04 Aug. 2016. Web. http://fortune.com/2016/08/05/5-things-you-need-to-know-about-donald-trumps-tax-returns/

[10] Smith, Allan. "Mark Cuban Lays out Why He Believes Donald Trump 'won't and Can't' Release His Taxes."*Business Insider*. Business Insider, Inc, 31 Aug. 2016. Web. <http://www.businessinsider.com/mark-cuban-donald-trump-tax-returns-2016-8>.

CHAPTER 15 – TRUMP AND HIS BUSINESSES

[1] Barsky, Neil. "Trump, the Bad, Bad Businessman." *The New York Times*. The New York Times, 06 Aug. 2016. Web. <http://www.nytimes.com/2016/08/07/opinion/sunday/trump-the-bad-bad-businessman.html>.

[2] Mair, Liz. "Donald Trump Is A Mediocre Businessman, And His Record Proves It."*Independent Journal Review*. N.p., 14 Sept. 2015. Web. <http://ijr.com/opinion/2015/09/247749-donald-trump-is-a-mediocre-businessman-and-his-record-proves-it/>.

[3] Isidore, Chris. "Donald Trump Bankruptcy: Everything You Want to Know."*CNNMoney*. Cable News Network, 31 Aug. 2015. <http://money.cnn.com/2015/08/31/news/companies/donald-trump-bankruptcy/index.html>.

[4] Date, S.V. "The 1 Easy Way Donald Trump Could Have Been Even Richer: Doing Nothing." *National Journal*. N.p., n.d. Web. <https://www.nationaljournal.com/s/54699/1-easy-way-donald-trump-could-have-been-even-richer-doing-nothing>.

[5] Eichenwald, Kurt. "Donald Trump's Business Failures: A Comprehensive Guide."*Newsweek*. N.p., 11 Aug. 2016. Web. <http://www.newsweek.com/2016/08/12/donald-trumps-business-failures-election-2016-486091.html>.

[6] IBID

CHAPTER 16 – TRUMP AND THE DISABLED

[1] Kessler, Glenn. "Donald Trump's Revisionist History of Mocking a Disabled Reporter."*Washington Post*. The Washington Post, 2 Aug. 2016. Web. <https://www.washingtonpost.com/news/fact-checker/wp/2016/08/02/donald-trumps-revisionist-history-of-mocking-a-disabled-reporter/>.

[2] Resnick, Gideon. *The Daily Beast*. Newsweek/Daily Beast, 2 Dec. 2015. Web. <http://www.thedailybeast.com/articles/2015/12/02/donald-trump-s-war-on-people-with-disabilities.html>.

CHAPTER 17 - TRUMP, PSYCHOPATHOLOGY AND THE NUCLEAR CODES

[1] Alford, Henry. "Is Donald Trump Actually a Narcissist? Therapists Weigh In!"*The Hive*. N.p., 11 Nov. 2015. Web. <http://www.vanityfair.com/news/2015/11/donald-trump-narcissism-therapists>.

[2] McAdams, Dan P. "THE MIND OF DONALD TRUMP." *The Atlantic*. Atlantic Media Company, June 2016. Web. <http://www.theatlantic.com/magazine/archive/2016/06/the-mind-of-donald-trump/480771/>.

[3] Behary, Wendy T. *Disarming the Narcissist: Surviving and Thriving with the Self-absorbed*. Oakland, CA: New Harbinger Publications, 2013. Print.

[4] News, BBC. "Trump Presidency Rated among Top 10 Global Risks: EIU." *BBC News*. N.p., 17 Mar. 2016. Web. <http://www.bbc.com/news/business-35828747>.

CHAPTER 18 – TRUMP AND HIS WORDS

[1] Cusack, Kevin Cirilli and Bob. "Trump: Economic Bubble about to Burst."*TheHill*. N.p., 14 Oct. 2015. Web. <http://thehill.com/homenews/campaign/256851-trump-economic-bubble-about-to-burst>.

CHAPTER 19 TRUMP, BIGOTRY, XENOPHOBIA AND RACISM

[1] Qui, Linda. "Donald Trump's Absurd Claim That He Knows Nothing about Former KKK Leader David Duke." *@politifact*. N.p., 2 Mar. 2016. Web. http://www.politifact.com/truth-o-meter/statements/2016/mar/02/donald-trump/trumps-absurd-claim-he-knows-nothing-about-former-/

[2] Totenberg, Nina. "Who Is Judge Gonzalo Curiel, The Man Trump Attacked For His Mexican Ancestry?" *NPR*. NPR, 7 June 2016. Web. http://www.npr.org/2016/06/07/481140881/who-is-judge-gonzalo-curiel-the-man-trump-attacked-for-his-mexican-ancestry

[3] Politi, Daniel. "Trump Tweets (Then Deletes) Image of Clinton, a Pile of Money, and Star of David." *Slate Magazine*. N.p., 02 July 2016. Web. <http://www.slate.com/blogs/the_slatest/2016/07/02/trump_tweets_image_of_clinton_a_pile_of_money_and_star_of_david.html>.

[4] IBID

[5] O'Donnell, John R., and James Rutherford. *Trumped!: The inside Story of the Real Donald Trump--his Cunning Rise and Spectacular Fall*. New York: Simon & Schuster, 1991. Print.

[6] Roberts, Dan. "Donald Trump's Legacy Threatens to Be Return of Race Politics to the Mainstream." *The Guardian*. Guardian News and Media, 27 Aug. 2016. Web. <https://www.theguardian.com/us-news/2016/aug/27/donald-trump-legacy-race-politics-mainstream>.

CHAPTER 20 – TRUMP AND THE ECONOMY

[1] Woodward, Bob, and Robert Costa. "In a Revealing Interview, Trump Predicts a 'massive Recession' but Intends to Eliminate the National Debt in 8 Years. "*Washington Post*. The Washington Post, 2 Apr. 2016. Web. <https://www.washingtonpost.com/politics/in-turmoil-or-triumph-donald-trump-stands-alone/2016/04/02/8c0619b6-f8d6-11e5-a3ce-f06b5ba21f33_story.html>.

[2] Goldmacher, Shane. "Trump Launches Tax Plan Rewrite." *POLITICO*. N.p., 11 May 2016. Web. http://www.politico.com/story/2016/05/donald-trump-taxes-tax-reform-223041

[3] Becker, Bernie. "Analysis Undercuts Trump's Claim That His Tax Plan Would Cost Him." *POLITICO*. N.p., 22 Dec. 2015. Web. <http://www.politico.com/story/2015/12/trump-tax-plan-analysis-217069>.

[4] McCaskill, Nolan. "Moody's Analytics Analysis: Trump Presidency Would 'significantly' Hurt Economy." *POLITICO*. N.p., 20 June 2016. Web. <http://www.politico.com/story/2016/06/trump-economy-moodys-analysis-224535>.

CHAPTER 21 – TRUMP AND HIS DOCTOR

[1] Blake, Aaron. "The Strange Tale of Donald Trump's Doctor Letter Just Got Stranger." *Washington Post*. The Washington Post, 27 Aug. 2016. Web. https://www.washingtonpost.com/news/the-fix/wp/2016/08/27/the-strange-tale-of-donald-trumps-doctor-letter-just-got-stranger/

[2] Healy, Patrick. "Hillary Clinton and Donald Trump, Ages 68 and 70, Share Few Health Details." *The New York Times*. The New York Times, 22 Aug. 2016. Web. http://www.nytimes.com/2016/08/23/us/politics/clinton-trump-health.html

[3] Blake, Aaron. "The Strange Tale of Donald Trump's Doctor Letter Just Got Stranger." *Washington Post*. The Washington Post, 27 Aug. 2016. Web. https://www.washingtonpost.com/news/the-fix/wp/2016/08/27/the-strange-tale-of-donald-trumps-doctor-letter-just-got-stranger/

CHAPTER 22 – TRUMP AND THE LOUSIANNA FLOODING

[1] Fahrenthold, David A. "Donald Trump Did Donate a Truckload of Supplies in La., and Intends to Write a $100,000 Check, His Campaign Says."*Washington Post*. The Washington Post, 24 Aug. 2016. Web. <https://www.washingtonpost.com/news/post-politics/wp/2016/08/23/did-donald-trump-make-donations-for-flood-relief-in-louisiana-heres-what-we-know/>

www.ingramcontent.com/pod-product-compliance
Lightning Source LLC
Chambersburg PA
CBHW080357030426
42334CB00024B/2909